Louis XIV and Richelieu

CLAUDIUS MOLLOKWU

authorHOUSE®

AuthorHouse™ UK
1663 Liberty Drive
Bloomington, IN 47403 USA
www.authorhouse.co.uk
Phone: UK TFN: 0800 0148641 (Toll Free inside the UK)
UK Local: (02) 0369 56322 (+44 20 3695 6322 from outside the UK)

© 2022 Claudius Mollokwu. All rights reserved.

No part of this book may be reproduced, stored in a retrieval system, or transmitted by any means without the written permission of the author.

Published by AuthorHouse 07/07/2022

ISBN: 978-1-6655-9986-3 (sc)
ISBN: 978-1-6655-9985-6 (e)

Print information available on the last page.

Any people depicted in stock imagery provided by Getty Images are models, and such images are being used for illustrative purposes only.
Certain stock imagery © Getty Images.

This book is printed on acid-free paper.

Because of the dynamic nature of the Internet, any web addresses or links contained in this book may have changed since publication and may no longer be valid. The views expressed in this work are solely those of the author and do not necessarily reflect the views of the publisher, and the publisher hereby disclaims any responsibility for them.

LOUIS XIV

Preface vii

Chapter 1   Early Years 1
Chapter 2   Consecration 17
Chapter 3   Louis and Absolutism 25
Chapter 4   Louis at Versailles 61
Chapter 5   Louis and Religion 75
Chapter 6   Foreign Policy 87

Concluding thoughts 95
Bibliography 99

PREFACE

I first encountered King Louis xiv of France during my A Level History studies. After a brief excursion from History, taken up as it were by my studies in Law, I soon encountered Louis once again during my Masters degree in History.

This monograph is an attempt to discuss and explore the issues concerning Louis of France's reign. Louis is regarded as one of the greatest monarchs that France has ever had, on a par with the likes of Napoleon Bonaparte and de Gaulle, both of whom he anticipated. In many ways they are all alike- all ruled untouched by any significant opposition, bar Louis' encounter with the frondeurs, all made important changes to French society, all modernised France albeit in their own unique ways- France and all enjoyed success in foreign adventures making France a global sphere and a global power.

It is generally noted amongst historians of the period that Louis was the first monarch in Europe to practice 'absolutism' which was to influence generations of later French monarchs. Many historians blame Louis's system of absolutism for causing the French revolution. Any view of Louis as an absolutist who assumed total control of France has been debunked. New generations of historians such as Nicholas Henshall, Geoffrey Treasure, John B Wolf, Arthur Hassall and Peter Robert Campbell credit Louis with being a collaborator and delegator who trusted his lieutenants- as it were to govern France. Far from being an absolutist monarch, one could note- albeit provisionally, that Louis was a democrat through his reforms to the political process, his adoption of the model of constitutional monarchy, his administrative and economic reforms and his reforms to the legal system (cf. Treasure, Louis xiv, Wolf, Louis xiv, Hassall, Louis xiv, Campbell, Louis xiv).

As well as his domestic reforms, Louis was a success internationally. By the end of his rule, France's borders and territories had substantively increased culminating with a member of the House of Bourbon- Louis' family occupying the Spanish throne.

Louis can be said to be the first person to create a nation state out of France. Through his reforms, political, administrative, economic, legal and religious, he gave France an identity and a self confidence that had previously eluded her. Beginning with his father, Louis xiii as well as the Roman Catholic cardinals, Richelieu and his protege Mazarin as well as Louis himself, France became powerful and became the leading country of Europe.

The monograph deals with Louis from a thematic approach where I address and discuss the main concerns of Louis' reign and rule.

This book is a work about a king who turned his country through his hard work and diligence into a successful and enviable power that was to set the trajectory of France on the path to prosperity and success.

I hope you enjoy it.

CHAPTER 1

Early Years

Louis XIV was born on the 5th September, 1638 at the royal palace in the Chateau de Saint-Germain-en-Laye to King Louis xiii of France of the House of Bourbon and Anne of Austria born in Spain and a member of the illustrious House of Hapsburg (cf. Bremond, La Provence Mystique au xvlle siècle, Wilkinson, Louis xiv, Treasure, Louis xiv). Louis was half French, half Spanish. He was named, Louis Dieudonne – Louis the God-given and assumed as was custom the title of 'Dauphin' (Bluche, 1990). He was Louis' and Anne's first child (cf. Petrie, Louis xiv). Louis birth was greeted with much enthusiasm by his parents and the people of France. Expectations were high for the new king:

As the Venetian Ambassador Angelo Carrario noted, 'This morning, a little before twelve o'clock, the

Queen, by an auspicious delivery, has enriched France with a Dauphin. The King together with his brother, the Princesses of the Blood and some of the great officers of the Crown…chose to assist her throughout, supporting her for a long time in his own arms. On perceiving the infant to be as fine a one and as healthy and well formed as could be desired, he immediately proceeded to the Church…and after a Te Deum had been chanted…. he returned to the Queens's apartments' (cf. Dunlop, Louis xiv).

Carrario continues: 'The joy of the people is boundless…throughout the city one walks through fire, and in many places, principally in the houses of the aristocracy, fountains of wine are seen to flow, thus increasing the gladness of men's hearts; nothing is heard but shouts of joy and congratulations' (cf. Dunlop, Louis xiv).

Richelieu himself noted- 'such great rejoicings as these, for this new favour shown to Heaven to the Kingdom of France, were never seen before' (cf. Dunlop, Louis xiv).

Anne soon adapted to her host country, France with ease and aplomb- assimilating herself into French society. On the day of her accession to the throne, she wore her earrings in the style of the French fleur-de-lys noting that she 'wanted everything to be French' (cf. Cronin, Louis xiv). She acquiesced to the kings demands to send away her Spanish 'maids, confessors, cooks and doctors' (cf. Cronin, Louis xiv). According to the historian, Maurice Ashley Louis and Anne's relationship was not a happy one. The birth of their first child took a long 23 years into their relationship before Lois was born- such was the lack of intimacy between the two (cf. Ashley, Louis and the Greatness of France). This view is supported by another historian, Richard Wilkinson who notes that they were 'incompatible, experiencing a distant, disfunctional relationship'- setting the scene for an unhappy marriage and an unhappy union (cf. Wilkinson, Louis xiv). Both Louis and Anne were cousins- they married at age the seventeen (cf. Cronin, Louis xiv).

Louis' name was significant, shared with many successful monarchs of France. Louis, was the name of the son of the holy roman emperor, Charlemagne, considered to be one of the most successful emperors in the history of Christendom, known for uniting Europe. There was another Louis- Louis the Lion, who had gained much territory for France from the English- his son was a crusader and a saint. Meanwhile, Louis xii was one of the best kings France had ever had (cf. Cronin, Louis xiv). Louis also shared the same name with France's only canonised saint-king, Louis ix.

Meanwhile, a few days later, just across France, in Spain, Anne's brother, Louis' uncle, Philip iv and his wife,

Louis' aunt, Elizabeth of the House of Bourbon gave birth to a girl, Maria Theresa. Both France and Spain had cause for joy- for both the Bourbon and Hapsburg enjoyed a significant presence in Europe by occupying the two major countries Europe- France and Spain. This caused Chavignovy, one of Richelieu's most influential ministers to note that 'the coincidence of the two births, might bring about, one day a great union and a great blessing to Christendom' (cf. Treasure, Louis xiv). His comment was to prove prophetic, anticipating the marriage between Louis and his cousin Maria Theresa.

Louis was special- surrounded by greatness as it were-he was half Bourbon and half Habsburg- both illustrious families of France and Spain- he was mixed race- half French and half Spanish. 'Of fourteen immediate ancestors, all but two had worn crowns. Further back were the Emperors Charles V and Maximilian. From the Medicis the child might inherit a taste for the arts, but also perhaps a touch of violence. Hapsburg blood would come to [Louis] from Anne of Austria, who was the daughter of two Hapsburgs, and from Marie de Medicis, whose mother was the Archduchess Joanna of Austria, Bourbon blood would come through the child's grandfather, Henri iv, who, through his father, Antoine Bourbon, was a direct descendant of Robert de Clermont, sixth son of St Louis' (cf. Cronin, Louis xiv). The pedigree of Louis' ancestors anticipated the importance that Louis would occupy in Europe. Louis was fully European, fully catholic and significantly of importance. Louis' birth was received with much joy and positive anticipation where leading contemporaries regarded him as gifted, a divine gift and his birth a miracle of God (cf. Barentine, 2016).

The Te Deum which greeted Louis' birth lasted in Paris for six consecutive days- such were the high hopes and goodwill that Louis was met with. As Cronin notes, there were fireworks, 'muskets and cannon salvoes and dancing in the streets'. Meanwhile in Saint-German, the place of the dauphin's birth, free wine sprung forth from the statues of four silver dolphins. At Lyons there were many fireworks, so much so 'that the air, infected by the plague which had recently swept this powerful city, was cleansed of impurities'. Even as far as Rome, Italy which anticipated the pope's bestowal of the title of Europe's 'most Christian king' and 'Eldest son of the Church' upon the dauphin celebrated the prince's birth with a Te Deum, sung in the church of 'Our Lady of Loretto', to which Anne returned the favour by granting the church a golden statute of her son (cf. Cronin, Louis xiv).

Gifts flooded the royal household. Pope Urban viii sent 'swaddling clothes, sheets pillow-cases, [and] bonnets…[from the New France Indians] there arrived at

Saint-Germain for the heir apparent the beaded outfit of a Redskin Papoose' (cf. Cronin, Louis xiv).

Louis and his mother, Anne were especially close enjoying a warm and loving relationship. Contemporaries and eyewitnesses claimed that the queen spent all of her free time with the dauphin (cf. Panhuysen, 2016). Both mother and son, had much in common and had shared interests. For example, both were interested in food and theatre. The closeness of their relationship is noted in Louis' journal entries:

'Nature was responsible for the first knots which tied me to my mother'.

Anne took a keen interest in her son's intellectual, cultural and spiritual development. In play and talk, she kept Louis company (cf. Treasure, Louis xiv).

Preceding the main event of his baptism, Louis was provisionally baptised at the time of his birth at the little oratory at the king and queen's apartments at the Chateau Neuf at Saint-German. Louis's baptism was unusually early, where he was baptised at the age of five on 21st April, 1643 rather than the required age of reason at seven. The baptism was held at the royal chapel at the Vieux Chateau. Cardinal Mazarin, soon to be Louis's first and last chief minister, draped in his magisterial crimson red and his cardinal's hat was in attendance and was his god-father- the Princesse de Conde, Charlotte de Montemorency was his god-mother. The Bishop of Meaux, Dominque Seguier, presided over the service (cf. Cronin, Louis xiv, Dunlop, Louis xiv).

Wilkinson notes that Louis, the dauphin's father was far from conventional. His physical health was poor having been wrecked by his doctors and their resulting negligence, his mental health wrecked by his father, Henri IV. This has been rebutted by the likes of Cronin, who notes that Louis was the 'opposite of Henri iv, his father, who had been a jolly, back-slapping fellow, physically strong and a born leader. [In contrast], Louis xiii was a gentle, quiet, reserved, extremely sensitive man, neither quick nor very intelligent and rather inclined to suspicion'. Louis xiii had a talent for administration where in an inspired act he employed the Catholic Cardinal, Richelieu as his first minister (cf. Cronin, Louis xiv). Their relationship- both king and cardinal was successful with Richelieu's being the 'the King's other self'. Richelieu sought to 'crush the nobles, crush the Huguenots [and] crush the house of Austria' (cf. Cronin, Louis xiv). Richelieu delivered much success to France- making France a proto-nation state which would be seen to completion with the reign of Louis xiv. The two were close-both king and cardinal corresponded every night where the king would confide in his cardinal (cf. Cronin, Louis xiv)- such was their closeness. According to the king's contemporary, La

Rochefoucauld, Louis took his cardinal's advice seriously- 'he never ceased to bend to the cardinal's will' (cf. Goethe and Harper, Louis xiv: The Real Sun King).

Soon, an illness befell Louis' father- he was suffering from 'tuberculosis of the digestive tract with acute tubercular peritonitis'. The king was brave, not letting his illness get the better of him. For example, he composed a fresh setting of the 'De Profundis' to be performed at his tomb. On Wednesday, the 14th May, 1643, Ascension Day, the king asked the queen's doctor how long he had left to live- Seguin replied, 'Sire, Your Majesty might have two or three hours at the most'. Anne, his wife knelt beside him and burst into tears. 'She loved the King more than she had imagined' and her fellow ladies escorted her from the king's bedside sobbing for the loss of her husband, the king (cf. Cronin, Louis xiv, Treasure, Louis xiv). The death of Louis' father, ushered in the regency era where his mother, Anne of Austria took on the responsibilities of governing France (cf. Wilkinson, Louis XIV).

Louis had cancelled the regency in his will. Instead a regency council of five was to be established curtailing his wife, Anne's powers. After appealing to Parliament Anne managed to secure a nullification of Louis' will that had prevented a regency. Parliament accepted Anne as Regent, granting her full decision-making powers (cf. Wilkinson, Louis xiv).

Anne aware of her own weaknesses, set out to choose someone worthy who would govern with her on behalf of her son the dauphin. She was spoilt for choice- many talented people could fill the role. Her brother-in law- Monsieur was only thirty-five- young but not quite bright. He was poor at decision making- according to his wife, Monsieur took longer to make a decision than she did to have a child. This discounted him from the post. Next, there was the dauphin's cousin the Prince de Conde from the Princes of the Blood- however he was narrow-minded and financially preoccupied, caring only for his 'prerogatives and money'- he spent his past times 'checking his cook's accounts'. As for the duc de Vendome, Henri iv's illegitimate child- he was not clever enough and like his son Beaufort, he was more concerned with the health and state of his family than he was for the wellbeing of France. Meanwhile the nobles were full of self interest, concerned with 'provincial governorships, more estates, more servants, carriages, horses and jewels'- than for the health of France. As for the petty nobility- they would never be taken seriously, given their minor status (cf. Cronin, Louis xiv).

By a process of elimination, Anne settled on her choice of Jules Mazarin, a roman catholic cardinal. He was Italian, born to his father, Pietro Mazzarino, a Sicilian a servant, whilst his mother, Ortensia Bufalini, hailed from the Bufalini nobility. After being educated by the Jesuits, he took a doctorate in law before entering the Papal diplomatic service. Mazarin was most likely chosen because like his predecessor Richelieu he was a cardinal, keeping the French tradition of the church collaborating with the state (cf. Dethan, 1959) intact. As Richelieu's protégé he was already attune, experienced and knowledgeable enough in France's affairs both domestic and international. He was the best candidate for the role of First Minister. Mazarin was ready to help the Queen Mother govern France.

Anne was loyal to her new first minister and co-regent. She defended Mazarin by exiling and arresting those who plotted and conspired against him in 1643, including the Duke of Beaufort and Marie de Rohan (cf. Treasure, Louis xiv, Petitfis, 2002).

Together, Anne and Mazarin ruled over France for the best part of 11 years. Both were Spanish, and outsiders as it were situated and surrounded in a world populated by the French. The differences in language between these two heads of government and their people set an uneasy relationship which was difficult between the rulers and the ruled, hailing as they were from different backgrounds. The regency was one of mixed success. Mazarin sought to negotiate an end to the long running war between France and Habsburg Austrians and Spanish before the crown's money ran out, however he only 'half succeeded'. According to Wilkinson, domestically, Mazarin was just as unsuccessful. I do not agree. Mazarin handled the assault by Henri IV"s illegitimate child, the duc de Beaufort well- he dealt with the uprising with kindness and fairness. Rather than executing, Beaufort was imprisoned and was to later be a helpful agent to the monarchy. He also successfully oversaw and presided over the end of the Frondes. Meanwhile, offices for places in parliament were sold enlarging the royal coffers (cf. Wilkinson, Louis xiv).

Together in 1648, Anne and Mazarin completed the 'Treaty of Westphalia' which ended the Thirty Years War (cf. Beem 2018). The Treaty enacted Dutch independence from Spain, awarded independence to some of the German princes of the Holy Roman Empire and granted Sweden seats on the Imperial Diet (cf. Barentine, 2016). In a stroke of fortuitous luck France gained the most- she gained all Hapsburg lands and claims in Alsace. France's de facto sovereignty was gained in the Three Bishophorics of Metz, Verdum and Toul (cf. Dvornik, 1962). Meanwhile in a bid to escape Hapsburg control, the German states sought the protection of France which resulted in the 1658 League of the Rhine, leading to the diminishing of imperial power.

After the 'Treaty of Westphalia', the Frondes was launched in 1648, which was a rebellion by the nobles against the monarchy. There are differing views as to what precisely caused the revolt. Historians such as Richard Wilkinson supported by Josephine Wilkinson note that the nobles were protesting- albeit belatedly against Cardinal Richelieu's centralisation of powers where he pushed out the nobles from any meaningful role in the governance of France. Confronted with the growing centralisation of powers- the nobles revolted in a bid to regain their lost powers (cf. Wilkinson, Louis xiv: The Real King of Versailles). Richelieu rather than working with members of the nobility was selective in those he chose to govern with- that is to say, his 'creatures'. Furthermore, 'his use of intendants annoyed France's 45,000 office-holders'. There's an alternative view- according to the historian Wilkinson he attributes the frondes to the rise of Mazarin, none of whom the frondeurs liked. For example, the frondeur Paul de Condi noted: 'Richelieu I disliked but respected; Mazarin I neither liked nor respected'. According to Wilkinson, Anne and Mazarin were responsible for the frondes as opposed to Richelieu. According to this view, Anne and Mazarin sidelined the nobility, 'alienat[ing] the aristocracy, the peasants, the city of Paris and the government's most reliable supporters, the office-holders' (cf. Wilkinson, Louis xiv). Upon this interpretation fault lies at the hands of Anne and Mazarin. According to Cronin, the frondes was a rebellion against Mazarin and not the king. Cronin continues: the frondes was a friendly war- even a family affair given that it included Louis' cousin, Prince de Conti who was Conde's youngest brother, as well as his supporters who included 'Conde's [] sister, Genevieve de Lonqueville, her husband, and her lover, the future Duc de La Rochefoucauld, as well as Duc de Beaufort' (cf. Cronin, Louis xiv). According to Magill the frondes were caused as a result of the government's desire to increase levels of taxation. This was rejected by parliament who 'questioned the constitutionality of the king's actions and sought to check his powers' (cf. Magill, Magill's History of Europe) consequentially launching a rebellion against the king.

There was a second frondes which ran from 1650 to 1653. This time, the nobility were concerned about their diminishing powers and their diminishing influence. They sought to protect their interests, launching a rebellion to protect said interest. Amongst the second frondeurs included 'the king's uncle Gaston, Duc of Orleans, his first cousin Anne-Marie Louis d'Orleans, Duchess of Montpensior, the princes such as Conde, his brother Armand de Bourbon, prince of Conti, and their sister the Duchess of Longueville, dukes of legitimised royal descent, such as Henri, Duke of Longueville and Francois, Duke of Beaufort, so called foreign princes, such as Frederic Maurice, Duke of Boullion, his mother Marshal Turenne, and Marie de Rohan, Duchess of

Chevreuse, and scions of France's oldest families, such as Francois de La Rochefoucauld'. Contrary to the common view, according to Wilkinson, Louis took the revolt well and forgave the nobles- 'I welcome you back and wish to forget your disloyalty'. (cf. Wilkinson, Louis xiv). Some historians have advanced the view that the frondes lies at the very heart of Louis' absolutism. According to this view, Louis believed that the frondes were caused by the monarchy not keeping tabs on the nobility hence they needed to be kept in check. The very laxity of the monarchy in dealing with the nobility led to the civil war. Louis sought to centralise powers and keep the nobility at court in Versailles where he could keep a close eye on them, preventing any further rebellions. However one could argue that Louis learnt the lessons of the frondes and ameliorated many of the nobles' concerns, by including them in the governance of France collaborating with them and delegating many of his powers to members of the nobility as well as to others from the Estates. I prefer the latter view.

Meanwhile, on 28th October 1649, in the month after Loui's seventh birthday, Anne noted to the Jesuit father, Florent de Montmorency, 'The king, my son, having by the grace of God, arrived at an age when it is necessary to begin to give him a Director of Conscience, in order that he may be able as soon as possible to adopt a way of life which conforms with the title, which is his by birth, of His Most Christian Majesty and the Eldest Son of the Church, I remembered having given my word to the fathers of your company that, when the time came, I would make my choice from among them'. She chose, Pere Paulin as Louis' spiritual director who was impressed by the young Louis- 'indeed, no lamb could be more meek and tractable than our King'. La Porte noted of the king that he was 'very ready to learn and yields always to reason'. On Christmas day, Louis and his brother Phillipe, now known as le petit Monsieur received their first communion at the Midnight Mass in the Church of Saint-Eustache. Together they had been confirmed a month earlier at the private chapel of the Palais-Royal. The 'young king', wrote the reporter to the Gazette, 'showed many signs of a great inclination to piety"' (cf. Dunlop, Louis xiv). Louis' training in matters of religion was to last him for the rest of his reign as king. He assumed and developed the concept of the 'divine right of kings' where he justified his position as king on the basis of being appointed by god to act as his sovereign majesty and sovereign ruler on earth. Meanwhile he firmly believed in 'the king's touch' where people who came into contact with the king would be miraculously healed. Louis remained a devout Roman catholic, loyal to the church and her institutions for the remainder of his reign.

CHAPTER 2

Consecration

At the age of fifteen, Louis participated in the 'Le Sacre'. He was consecrated and crowned as King (cf. Wilkinson, Louis xiv). The sacre was anticipated with much excitement- 'we have great and high hopes that something good will come from the sacre', noted Guy Patin, Dean of the Faculty of Medicine at the Sorbonne. The ceremony took place at Reim Cathedral on 7th June 1654 (cf. Wilkinson, Louis xiv). It had been delayed by two years due to the trouble with the frondes as well as France's war with Spain (cf. Cronin, Louis xiv). In attendance at the ceremony were Anne, his mother and Mazarin, his chief minister. The procession into the church consisted of the grand Provost of France, 'followed by…trumpeters' and musicians dressed in 'white tafetta', representatives of every province 'dressed in velvet, with white silk stockings' their clothes 'embroidered with fleurs de lys', the 'gentlemen called raven-breaks, and the Marquis de Rhodes, and the Constable, Marechal d'Etrees' surrounded by 'two ushers carrying the gilt mace' (cf. Cronin, Louis xiv)

The King followed, proceeding his Chancellor (cf. Cronin, Louis xiv). He was greeted by lay and spiritual peers with cries of: 'Vivat rex in aeternum'- 'May the King live forever'.

Before the Bishop of Soissons who officiated at the ceremony, Louis promised to 'defend and observe the rights of the Catholic Church'. He also promised to govern well on behalf of his people, and would protect his people from all harm (cf. Wilkinson, Louis xiv):

Louis partook in the sacraments of the church. As Cronin notes, the Bishop of Soissons, dipped his thumb in the balm and proceeded to anoint the king with the oil of clovis in seven places 'brow, chest, between the shoulders, right shoulder, left shoulder, bend of the right arm and bend of the left arm. The crosses of oil were left moist on the King's body' (cf. Cronin, Louis xiv, Wilkinson, Louis xiv). As Cronin notes anthems and prayers followed which heralded Louis as the successor of 'Saul, David and Solomon', signalling his importance (cf. Cronin, Louis xiv). Louis was robed in 'tunic, dalmatic' and striking velvet. According to Cronin, the similarity to the bishops vestments could signify Louis' role as both layman and priest. Another interpretation is that Louis' robes resembled the vestments of the byzantine emperors, from whom the coronation rights of Christian kings hailed from (cf. Cronin, Louis xiv).

The bishop also placed a ring on Louis' third finger, signifying his everlasting covenantal marriage to France and her people (cf. Cronin, Louis xiv, Wilkinson, Louis xiv). Next, Louis was crowned with the Crown of Charlamagne, the great king who unified Europe ruling 'not only France, but also the Low Countries, Austria, half Germany and half Italy'. As the Pope had designated Charlemagne 'Emperor of the West' he was the legitimate heir and 'successor of Augustus, Trajan and Constantine'. By receiving Charlemagne's crown, Louis was aping and anticipating the greatness that his reign would bring France aping the role that Charlemagne had once occupied (cf. Cronin, Louis xiv). Louis was the new Charlemagne. Louis then bearing his crown and sceptre, took to the throne, where he was greeted with kisses from the peers. Louis was also given Charlemagne's sword-probably to signify his military might. The bishop hailed the new king 'May the King live for ever!' (cf. Cronin, Louis xiv).

After the Te Deum was chanted, Mass then took place. Louis also took confession and received holy communion. After Mass, wearing a light crown filled with 'pearls and diamonds he walked in procession down the nave to the west door, while bells rang and the organ pealed, to be seen and hailed by his subjects' (cf. Cronin, Louis xiv). Within Louis, there was a union of church, state and the French. Louis was devoted to the church, which had bequeathed to him the titles of 'Most Christian King' and 'Eldest Son of the Church' (cf. Wilkinson, Louis xiv). Emboldened by the papacy's support, Louis set out on the trajectory of establishing France as the leading Catholic nation.

According to Cronin, there are seven reasons which illuminate the reasons for Louis being crowned king of France.

First, Louis was now 'the anointed of the Lord' signifying his specialness and uniqueness. As the lawyer, Omer Talon puts it: 'Sire, the place where Your Majesty is seated represents for us the throne of the living God'.

Secondly, Louis was confirmed as the 'absolute ruler of some eighteen million subjects' As Restif de La Bretonne notes 'that the king could legally oblige every man to give his wife or daughter, and my whole village- Sacy in Burgundy- thought as I did'. Louis absolutism was derived from the divine right of kings, leading one to commentator to note, 'it belongs not the subjects, either to create or censure but to honour and obey their sovereign, who comes to be so by a fundamental hereditary right

Louis XIV and Richelieu

of succession, which no religion, no law, no fault or forfeiture can alter or diminish'. As Cronin notes, some held the view the king's powers were checked where the likes of the theorists such as Jean Bodin noted that the king's powers were kept in checked by the laws of God and nature and by the very constitutionality of the state. Meanwhile, others have noted that the king was free from restraint. According to Cronin, the most popular view is that the king's powers was kept in check by an account of Christian principles. As the former Coajudtor of Paris who was made a cardinal by louis notes, 'Sire, your rule will be like that of God, because your power will have no limits but those which you yourself impose in accordance with justice and reason'.

Third, Louis was- as it were the spiritual director of his people, taking seriously the spiritual life of his people which was entrusted to him. Louis had the role of appointing all but a 'few archbishops, bishops and abbots' (cf. Cronin, Louis xiv) which he took seriously ensuring that his people had access to talented and gifted clergy.

Fourth, Louis was king of an entity and a concept called France. To be a king of France, up till the point when Louis became king was to be in charge of a few disparate provinces. Louis was arguably the first king to rule a united France that was cohesive and comprehensive and was one of the first nation states.

Fifth, Louis was the very 'personification of France' (cf. Cronin, Louis xiv). In a sense he was 'France incarnated'. Louis identification with France can be summed up in his maxim 'L'etat c'est moi', translated as 'I am the State'- or rather 'I am France' (cf. Church, The Greatness of Louis xiv).

Sixth, Louis was 'a demi-god' which derives in a sense from his governance and identification of his rule being legitimated by the 'divine right of kings'. His cousin, Mademoiselle noted that "the King is like a god', while a trained lawyer Omer Taylon noted that the 'king belongs to the race of gods'. Evelyn noted that the 'French are the only nation in Europe to idolise their sovereign' (cf. Cronin, Louis xiv).

Last of all, the king was designated as the sovereign protector of his people, protecting 'them from oppression and injustice' (cf. Cronin, Louis xiv). In that sense, Louis could be considered to be one of the first enlightened despots who governed on behalf of the wellbeing of his people, taking their concerns seriously and aimed to deal with such concerns. Louis anticipated and set the standard and was the model for enlightened rulers that followed such as Frederick of Prussia, Peter the Great and Catherine the Great both of Russia (cf. Oppenheimer, Enlightened Despots, Massie, Peter the Great, Massie,

Louis XIV and Richelieu

Catherine the Great, Simon Sebag-Montefiore, The Romanovs, Catherine and Potemkin).

The coronation and festivities ended with the gift of the king to his people where he released some six hundred prisoners.

It was at this time that Louis began looking for a lover and a wife. He was attracted to Marie Mancini, Mazarin's niece. However both Anne and Mazarin did not support Louis' choice and sent Mancini away from court to be married in Italy. Anne supported by Mazarin sought to arrange a marriage between her son Louis and her niece, Louis' first cousin, the Spanish Infanta, Maria Theresa of Spain, daughter of Phillip IV of Spain, the Queen Mother's brother. Maria was half Spanish, half Portuguese. Anne was ambitious- whereas Mancini was of minor nobility, the daughter of Philip of Spain came from the illustrious Hapsburg family. The idea of a union between the great House of Bourbon and the House of the Hapsburg was a masterstroke, inspired and audacious. The marriage between the consorts of France and Spain was to have a lasting impact and influence on France's relationship with her European cousins which still to this very day bears an imprint on the House of Bourbon. Maria Theresa married Louis, her double cousin in 1660, a year before Louis' personal rule of France (cf. Fraser, Love and Louis xiv: The Women in the Life of the King).

CHAPTER 3

Louis and Absolutism

'I have decided to take charge of the state in person'. And so Louis' personal rule began on 10th March, 1661, the day Mazarin passed away (cf. Treasure, Louis xiv) at the castle of Vincennes between 2 and 3 pm (cf. Cronin, Louis xiv).

Mazarin's death heralded the beginning of Louis' absolutism where he assumed absolute and total control of France. In this his absolutism Louis was supported by the French people. The French historian Ronald Mousnier notes that the general public approved and supported Louis' adoption of absolutism- 'Absolutism was the wish of the multitudes that sought their salvation in the consecration of power in the hands of a single man, who should be the incarnation of the realm and the living symbol of the desired order and unity. Everyone endeavoured to behold the image of God in the king: 'You are God on earth" (cf. Church, The Greatness of Louis xiv). That is the standard interpretation of Louis' rule. In this chapter I will seek to advance the view that Louis, rather than being dictatorial or a despot was actually a constitutional monarch who ruled in coalition and in collaboration with his ministers and members of the noblesse de robe and the noblesse d'eppee. Power was dispersed rather than concentrated. Contrary to Mousnier's view the French did not like absolutism- they revolted against that model during the first and second rebellions of the frondes. Louis learnt his lessons and sought to adopt the model of constitutional monarch where he included all to help him in his governance of France.

Mazarin was aged fifty-nine when he passed away. Was Mazarin, merely a stop gap and cool down, between Richelieu and Louis XIV, two great absolutists, or was he a pivotal figure, upon whom France depended on? It is arguably the latter. Like Richelieu, he served in office for the best part of eighteen years. Mazarin was a significant force in France. He negotiated the terms of the Treaty of Westphalia where France succeeded in gaining several territories from the Hapsburgs. The Treaty of the Pyrenees, another treaty which Mazarin negotiated confirmed France as the 'dominant western European power' replacing Spain in this regard. Mazarin also presided over the 'League of the Rhine' which protected Germany from 'Hapsburg encroachment' and negotiated The Treaty of Oliva which installed peace in the Baltic. He also made peace with Holland and England who became allies of France. Mazarin was a skilled negotiator, adept at handling and solving moments of crises in France's life. Mazarin was a success in terms of his foreign policy, where he bequeathed Louis a strong hand which Louis was to exploit with much success during his personal rule (cf. Wilkinson, Louis xiv) According to Treasure, 'Louis can be said to have fulfilled Mazarin's territorial hopes- and more' (cf. Treasure, Louis xiv).

Meanwhile, domestically, according to Wilkinson, Mazarin's record is more mixed. Of course France had survived the frondes- of which the credit lies with Mazarin as well as Anne. The Jansenist faction was defeated and silenced. Upon Mazarin's initiative Conde, the king's cousin and fourth in line for the throne (cf. Petrie, Louis xiv) abandoned the Spaniards and swore loyalty to Louis, pleading for Louis' pardon. In an inspired act, Mazarin granted Conde and the Princes of the Blood consultation rights over the affairs of state (cf. Mansel, King of the World). Those are the domestic and internal successes of Mazarin's rule. However, the peasants were subjected to over-taxation and suffered impoverishment. Agriculture remained unreformed. The finances of the royal government was stretched paying its 45,000 office-holders. Mazarin left the country, a crippling debt of 451 million Livres. Louis claimed in his memoirs that chaos and 'disorder reigned everywhere', such was Mazarin's incompetence. Financially, Mazarin handsomely gained from his role as first minister amassing a personal fortune of some 39 million counter to Richelieu's 22 million livres. If Richelieu's fortune was 'excessive' then Mazarin's fortune was 'obscene' attracting the ire of the French people. Nothing stood in the way of Mazarin's greed- 'abbeys, offices, jewels, pictures, medals, cash'- all were amassed and assumed by the cardinal (cf. Wilkinson, Louis xiv). To be fair to Mazarin, he bequeathed his fortune to Louis, paying back the state- as it were.

As Hassall notes, the Queen Mother after Louis xiv reached his seventh year, appointed Mazarin as the chief educator of her son, naming him 'Surintendant of the Education of the King'. Mazarin delegated the supervision of the dauphin's education to 'Villeroi, his governor, Perefixe his teacher, [later to become Archbishop of Paris], and La Porte his principal 'Valet-de-Chambre'. Madame de Monteville tells us the dauphin 'was taught to translate the commentaries of Caesar; he learnt to dance, to draw, and to ride, and he was very skilful at all athletic exercises'. He took a keen interest in history, and 'especially delighted in the wars of Charles the Great, St Louis, and

Francis I' (cf. Hassall, Louis xiv). For the last eight years of his life, Mazarin taught Louis the art of 'statecraft'. He engaged Louis in one to one sessions whilst they travelled together to 'inspect the army' or removed any opposition that stood in their way. Mazarin was impressed by his pupil's intelligence noting in a letter to Marshal Gramont, '[Louis] is worth four kings and a man of integrity as well'. He was pleased with the king's progress and had high expectations of Louis - 'It depends on you to become the most glorious king the world has ever seen'. He asked Louis to prioritise foreign policy as party of the king's 'gloire' where France, he believed should be the leading dominant European power. Perhaps Mazarin's greatest gift of all to Louis was his discovery of Jean-Baptiste Colbert, who was to become Louis' closest and favourite collaborator (cf. Wilkinson, Louis xiv). Mazarin at the end of his life is reported to have said to Louis: 'Sire, I owe you everything, but I believe I can repay some of my debt by giving you Colbert' (cf. Treasure, Louis xiv).

Mazarin and Louis were close. Mazarin taught Louis all that he needed to govern France. Louis, equipped by Mazarin, was ready to govern France.

At the death of Mazarin in 1661, Louis 'broke into tears: he had lost his guide, a faithful Minister and his best friend'. Louis was twenty-three and had been reigning for some eighteen years (cf. Hassall, Louis xiv). Louis quickly recollected himself:

'I felt quite another man. I discovered in myself qualities I had never suspected, and I joyfully rebuked myself for having been unaware of them so long. Like every reflective person I had suffered from timidity, especially when I had to speak at length in public, but this very soon disappeared. Only then did it seem to me that I was the king, born to be king' (cf. Wilkinson, Louis xiv).

Here Louis was quickly becoming aware of his potential to be a powerful king which anticipated though not yet in crystalised coherent form, his decision to be his own first minister.

After the death of Mazarin, Louis summoned what was to be his first Council where he addressed a gathering of just three ministers- 'Michael Le Tellier, aged fifty-eight, Secretary for War, a prudent, simple-living administrator from a legal family; Hugues de Lionne, aged fifty, Acting Secretary of State for Foreign Affairs, a widely experienced diplomat and for twenty years Mazarin's right-hand man; Nicholas Fouquet, aged forty six, Attorney-General and Superintendent of Finances, by birth a member of the high bourgeoisie, married in turn to two heiresses, a man of wealth and dazzling gifts'. The meeting lasted for two hours and was dispatched after concluding urgent business (cf. Wilkinson, Louis xiv). Together this coalition of ministers, with the exception of Fouquet would form the team of the king where he governed France in collaboration with all of the aforementioned, barring said Fouquet.

After the first council, Louis convened a second council where he followed the natural logic of his kingship in what was an audacious and inspired move, he decided to become his own chief minister. Present at this second council, in addition to Le Tellier, Lionne and Fouquet, was the seventy two year old Chancellor, the Comte de Brienne, the secretary of state for foreign affairs, Louis' boyhood friend and by two secretaries of state (cf. Cronin, Louis xiv).

Louis addressed the gathering:

'I have summoned you with my Ministers and Secretaries of State to tell you that until now I have been quite willing to let my affairs be managed by the late Cardinal; in future I shall be my own Prime Minister'.

'Monsieur, the Chancellor, I have called you, together with my secretaries and ministers of state, to tell you that up to this moment I have been pleased to entrust the government of my affairs to the late cardinal. It is now time that I govern them myself. You will assist me with you counsels, when I ask for them. Outside the regular business of justice which I do not intend to change, Monsieur the Chancellor, I request and order you to seal no orders except by my command, or after having discussed them with me, or at least not unless a secretary brings them to you on my part. And you, Messieurs, my secretaries of state. I order you not to sign anything, not even a passport, without my command, to render account to me personally each day and to favour no one. And you, Monsieur the Superintendent, I have explained to you my wishes; I request you to use M.Colbert whom the late Cardinal has recommended to me. As for Lionne, he his assured of my affection. I am satisfied with his services' (cf. Wilkinson, Louis xiv).

Louis' address signalled the birth of the doctrine of absolutism, necessary for his 'gloire'. Within the address contains the birth pangs of the doctrine of absolutism which was to set the trajectory of France for many centuries yet to come.

Louis was confident in his own abilities to rule France as his own first minister. On the same day as his second council, the Archbishop of Rouen at an audience with the king said 'Sire, I have the honour of presiding over the assembly of the clergy of your kingdom; Your Majesty ordered me to consult the Cardinal on all matters; he is now dead; to whom does Your Majesty wish that I should address myself in future?' Louis answered 'To me' (cf. Cronin, Louis xiv). According to Brienne, Secretary of

Louis XIV and Richelieu

State: 'He had decided to take charge of the state in person and to rely on no one else' (cf. Treasure, Louis xiv).

Louis' personal rule had begun.

The standard interpretation is that absolutism was the personal decision and idea of Louis envisaged and inspired by the frondes where Louis sought to rule France with an iron rod in order to prevent dissent from the nobles or any one else for that matter. With Louis' absolutism the governance of France was set on a trajectory that would last for a long time well into the nineteenth century and would prove to be the downfall of France with the occurrence of the French revolution which temporarily ended the royal House of Bourbon. Louis's embrace and adoption of absolutism and the doctrine of the 'divine right of kings' has been supported by Louis' contemporary, the historian and administrator Pierre-Edourd Lemontey: 'This monarchy was pure and absolute. It was centred entirely in royalty, and royalty was entirely in the king. The king mirrored the divinity and had a similar right to [] obedience' (cf. Church, The Greatness of Louis xiv).

What does the policy of absolutism entail? Well, put simply, it means that as king, Louis assumed absolute and total control of France. As the French historian, Louis Madelin notes' '[t]he state' was [Louis'] first preoccupation. 'The interest of the state should always take precedence' and besides, 'when one works for the state, one works for oneself. The good of the one enhances the glory of the other'. If [Louis] was the state, the state was France' (cf. Church, The Greatness of Louis xiv).

'L'etat c'est moi'- that is to say 'I am the State', or 'I am France' as it were was Louis' identification of himself as the state where he embodied and incarnated all that was best about France. Louis' fortunes were inextricably bound up with the fortunes of the state and ultimately of France. As part of his absolutism was the doctrine of the 'divine right of kings', Many scholars supported the doctrine. For example, Bossuet notes:

'[R]oyal authority is sacred…paternal…absolute…subject to reason…God establishes kings as His ministers and reigns over people through them…Therefore princes act as ministers of God and as His lieutenants on earth. It is through them that He exercises His empire…The person of the king is sacred…God has had them anointed by His prophets with a sacred ointment, as He has had His pontiffs and His altars anointed. But even before being in fact anointed, they are sacred by virtue of their task, as representatives of His divine majesty…delegated by His providence to execute His design…

Religion and conscience demand that we obey the prince…Even if kings fail in [their] duty, their charge and their ministry must be respected. For Scripture tell us: 'Obey your masters, not only those who are mild and good, but also those who are…unjust'. Thus there is something religious in the respect which one renders the prince. Service to God and respect for kings are one thing…

The prince need render account to no one for what he orders…When the prince has judged there is no other judgment' (cf. Mallia-Milanes).

Bossuet continues:

'It is God who establishes kings. He caused Saul and David to be anointed by Samuel; He vested royalty in the House of David, and ordered him to cause Solomon, his son, to reign in his place…

Princes thus act as ministers of God and His lieutenants on earth. It is through them that He rules… This is why we have seen that royal throne is not the throne of a man, but the throne of God himself…

It appears from this that the person of kings is sacred, and to move against them is sacrilege. God causes them to be anointed by the prophets with a sacred unction, as He caused the pontiffs and His altars to be anointed' (cf. Church, The Greatness of Louis xiv).

The concept of the divine right, contrary to opinion was not part of the absolutism of Louis- not quite- instead the doctrine can be said to be an enhancer of the model of constitutional monarchy which acted as a guiding principle for said model. The principle supported the 'primus inter pares' which describes and supplements the relationship with the king, his ministers and the nobility. Upon this interpretation Louis was appointed as sovereign ruler by god to govern France which he duly did in concert with his ministers, members of the nobility as well as leading figures of the church.

Contrary to popular and academic opinion, Louis was not an absolutist. That theory is over-'nonsense on stilts' as it were (cf. Bentham)- it is fiction. This view has most recently been supported by the historian, Peter Robert Campbell who notes that the attempted centralisation of power was only inchoate and incomplete faced by a hang up and hangover of a 'bastard feudalism' (cf. Campbell, Louis xiv). Louis was a collaborator. He surrounded himself with a strong team who worked with him. He was not afraid to delegate powers and responsibilities to his ministers- he trusted them to govern efficiently in his name. Louis had a talented generation of ministers- nobles included. As Saint-Simon notes Louis' 'ministers were the most skilful in all Europe; his generals were the best; his court was filled with illustrious and clever men'. According to Saint-Simon, Louis too was talented 'and was made for a brilliant court' (cf. Church, The Greatness of Louis xiv). According to Louis in his 'Memoirs', written when he was around thirty years old, his chosen ministers 'were destined not to govern but to serve the king' (cf.

Church, The Greatness of Louis xiv). Despite these earlier sentiments, Louis changed his mind and changed tack by delegating and allowing free rain to his ministers to govern in a manner that they saw fit. This view has been supported by the historian Pierre Goubert who notes 'as early as 1661, as he declared in his Memoires, Louis meant to have sole command in every sphere and claimed full responsibility, before the world and all posterity, for everything that should happen in his reign. In spite of constant hard work he soon found he had to entrust the actual running of certain departments, such as finance or commerce, to a few colleagues, although he still reserved the right to take major policy decisions himself' (cf. Church, The Greatness of Louis xiv).

After the false start of including Nicholas Fouquet, Louis recovered and appointed the likes of Colbert, Le Tellier, and Lionne to help him govern France. Louis was a delegator- he entrusted responsibility to his ministers and trusted them to get on with their work without further interference. As Wolf notes, Louis discussed his affairs with these three. He also met with secretaries of state, the chancellor and others who were vital to the business of France. Louis notes: 'I wished...to divide the execution of my orders among several people, the better to bring them under my authority. It was with this mind that chose men of diverse talents and professions, fitting the diversity of the materials that ordinarily fall under the administration of state, and I distributed my time and my confidence according to the understanding that I had of their virtues and the importance of the affairs that I gave over to them' (cf. Wolf, Louis xiv). Louis chose to surround himself with men of aptitude and intelligence.

The historian Vincent Cronin notes Bossuet's defence of Louis' choice to rule as a constitutional monarchy:

'According to Bossuet monarchy is the most usual, the oldest and the most natural form of government, being modelled on the family. It is also the best, because most opposed to division. Of all the monarchies the most perfect is the hereditary, especially from father to eldest son, because this is the form God established among his chosen people. A monarch must be reasonable, but should he happen to yield to irregularity, inconstancy, inequality or eccentricity, the people must continue to practise obedience; instead of criticising the form of government they must profit from the security it affords to lead Christian lives' (cf. Cronin, Louis xiv).

Louis took these principles on board but also stressed the necessity of the monarchy for the wellbeing and welfare of his people. 'A King' he wrote, 'must bring all classes of his subjects to the perfection befitting their nature'. 'When a King labours for himself; the welfare of the one constitutes the glory of the other. When the former is great, happy and powerful, he who is the cause of all these advantages is glorious' (cf. Wolf, Louis xiv). For Louis the interests of the king and the interests of his people coincide with one another and are both one and the same.

As Geoffrey Treasure notes, Fouquet was the discovery of Mazarin- though some say of Richelieu (cf. Treasure, Louis xiv), and was even tipped to become first minister of France. Fouquet was clever- he had wide-ranging interests. He 'wrote Latin verses and argued philology with the Jesuits'. He was a creative, suggesting 'themes to La Fontaine, Pierre and Thomas Corneille and Pellisson'. He was cultured- 'he collected prints, coins, statutes and rare manuscripts, The Orientalists Vatier and Barthelemy d'Herbelot, were in his pay'. He was also a talented historian and geographer. He took his family's motto seriously- 'To what heights will he not climb'. According to Cronin 'the devious Nicholas Fouquet wanted to know everything and to do everything' (cf. Cronin, Louis xiv). According to Treasure, Fouquet's ascendancy was swift- he 'had been promoted to high office unusually early'. At the age of 33 in 1650 he became 'procureur-general'. In 1653, Mazarin appointed him surintendant (cf. Treasure, Louis xiv).

Fouquet had a bright start. In 1657, when the army was suffering from funding issues, Fouquet rescued the day by raising nearly a million livres in four days. However despite such a confident start, it all went downhill. There is a disagreement at what caused Fouquet's downfall. Some historians such as Wilkinson and Treasure attribute Fouquet's downfall to due to his embezzlement and misappropriation of public funds (cf. Wilkinson, Louis xiv, Treasure, Louis xiv). Louis accused Fouquet of 'fortifying his properties adorning his palaces, forming cabals and securing key places for his friends, bought at my expense in the hope of making himself the sovereign arbiter of the state' (cf. Treasure, Louis xiv). By paying for private activities using public funds, Fouquet could be accused of the crime of embezzlement. According to Robert Briggs 'Fouquet was the victim of a frame-up by Colbert' and was to 'some extent [] a pre-emptive strike'. According to Wilkinson Fouquet's downfall began when Colbert informed the king that the visit by Louis to Le Vau where he was hosted by Fouquet was paid and funded not by Fouquet but by the king's very own funds. Louis was incensed and a few days later on the king's orders, Fouquet was arrested by D'Artagnan, the musketeer (cf. Wilkinson, Louis xiv). In other words, Colbert was just getting rid of the competition. Others such as Cronin have attributed the downfall of Fouquet to himself where he was not honest with the king over discrepancies concerning the state's expenditures and income, despite

Louis XIV and Richelieu

Louis' constant questioning of said discrepancies. An alternative view according to Cronin is that Fouquet's powers were growing beyond out of all control and posed a significant threat to the king's powers (cf. Cronin, Louis xiv) Fouquet was taking over the country- as Cronin notes, 'everywhere [Fouquet] had allies and spies, Lionne, Acting Secretary of State [, fast living like Fouquet was in Fouquet's] pay[roll], [as], [], Mademoiselle de Menneville, one of Anne's 'maids-of-honour, was Fouquet's mistress and supplied him with news in return for £50,000 which she used as a dowry to marry the Duc d'Amville. Madam de Beauvais also passed on palace secrets' (cf. Cronin, Louis xiv). Things could not continue this way- the king was being surrounded and threated in his own country- as Hassall notes, the king feared that Fouquet would interfere with his governance of France (cf. Hassall, Louis xiv). The king swiftly replied to the growing powers and influence of Fouquet and decided to sack him- in other words Louis was getting rid of a tyrant. On another interpretation, one could note that Fouquet fell out of favour because he was simply incompetent at dealing properly with the state's finances. After his arrest, a trial was held for three years before Fouquet was found guilty, banished from the kingdom where he was imprisoned at the castle of Pignerolo, on the borders of Piedmondt, for the remaining twelve years (cf. Dunlop, Louis xiv).

Fouquet was replaced by his rival and one time assistant, Colbert in September (cf. Treasure, Louis xiv).

According to Treasure, the downfall of Fouquet is related to Louis' decision to become his own first minister. With Fouquet out of the way, Louis had eliminated his premier centre of opposition. He capitalised on Fouquet's disgrace by centralising power and then distributing said power. With Fouquet out of the way, Louis was allowed to be himself- 'nothing can so securely establish the happiness and tranquillity of country as the perfect combination of all authority in the single person of the Sovereign' (cf. Cronin, Louis xiv). As Hassall notes, the removal of Fouquet signalled the end of an era and the end of the old order which had been dominated by Richelieu and Mazarin and their systems of governance (cf. Hassall, Louis xiv). With Fouquet out of the way, a new generation was born and had taken over

As the historian Geoffrey Treasure notes echoed by John B. Wolf, 'the word 'team' is appropriate' to denote the people that surrounded the king and governed in concert with him (cf. Treasure, Louis xiv, Wolf, Louis xiv). Far from being a dictator or an absolutist, Louis was a collaborator who knew when and how to delegate matters to his ministers. Louis streamlined his council from an unwieldy cabal to a royal council of four. The council of four at the outset was presided by Louis himself and included Mazarin's men in a spirt of continuity so as not to cause disruption to affairs of state. As the philosopher Leibnitz notes, 'Although the king [Louis xiv] no longer had a preceptor after the death of Cardinal Mazarin, he was governed for a time by the latter's maxims and counsels as though he were still living, especially as M.de Lionne was a product of this school and followed the same principles' (cf. Church, The Greatness of Louis xiv). Mazarin's men who became Louis' men included Le Tellier, Pomponne, Louvois and Colbert. Colbert was the last to join, given that he replaced the disgraced Fouquet. Colbert was responsible for finance, the navy, royal buildings and the king's lifestyle (cf. Wilkinson, Louis xiv). Despite Colbert being the last to join the council of four, Louis was to rely heavily upon Colbert who one could argue was Louis' de facto first minister in all but name. Councils were established in September 1661 where Colbert and Louis agreed that Louis would take the important decisions first before presenting his polices to the councils for their consideration and ratification. This model and agreement, as Treasure notes meant that Louis kept abreast of all affairs and all occurrences in his kingdom (cf. Treasure, Louis xiv, Wilkinson, Louis xiv). The councils heralded the birth of France's bureaucratic and administrative system. Louis devolved and delegated matters to each of his secretaries of state giving them creative freedom to act in their respective briefs.

As Wilkinson notes, 'various councils' were convened to govern France. The 'conseil d'en haut was the main council, so called 'because it always met at least twice a week on an upper floor'. The council included the aforementioned three secretaries of states. Louis led proceedings at the council d'en haut. Louis sporadically presided over the 'conseil des depeches' which met weekly and dealt with the 'internal affairs of France'. It included the chancellor and four secretaries of state- army, navy, foreign policy…each responsible for a section in the country. The Princes of the blood, cousins to Louis, such as Conde were granted rights to attend the council if they so wished. Louis headed the conseil de finances of which Colbert attended and was the key member. The conseil de commerce' which was Colbert's project was 'set up in 1664, [but] lapsed in 1677', only to reappear in 1700'. The conseil de parties was a legislative body which also 'acted as a court of appeal'. Though Louis did not chair these latter two councils he chaired the conseil de conscience which met every Friday morning. Here, Louis was accompanied by the archbishop of France and his confessor (cf. Wilkinson, Louis xiv).

Louis was determined to apply himself diligently to his new duties:

'I made it a rule to work regularly twice a day for two or three hours at a time with various persons, aside from the hours that I worked alone or that I might devote to extraordinary affairs if they arose. I command the four secretaries of state to sign nothing in future without discussing it with me, and the same for the superintendent of finances, and for nothing to be transacted in the finances without it being registered in a little book that was to remain with me. I resolved to enter into details with each of the ministers when he would least expect it' (cf. Wilkinson, Louis xiv).

The conseil d'en haut met four or five times a week and the other councils- three or four times. Louis for the most part chaired these meetings. He listened and took on board the views of his ministers and would often accept majority decisions made in the council. Louis' system of councils heralded the birth of a modern bureaucratic state comprised of councils, parliaments, the three estate-generals comprised of the aristocracy, the church and everyone else, as well as the system of the intendants. According to Mousnier, the king's reforms which often took power away from the nobility realised a state built not on social hierarchy or a society of classes but was one in which there was a transition 'from the absolute monarchy to the centralised bureaucratic state'. Whilst Mousnier has a point noting the transition of the state from one built on absolutist principles to a modern bureaucratic state (cf. Mallia-Milanes, Louis xvi and France) he is wrong to note that the nobles and old social orders were sidelined- on the contrary- they were included in the governance of France, advising the king on all sorts of matters of policy and all sorts of issues. For example, Conde and the princes of the blood were free to attend the conseils. France through Louis's administrative reforms gained an identify and a self-confidence supremely aware of her strengths. Louis' councils were filled with luminaries and stars. To them, we turn.

Jean Baptise Colbert was appointed to the king's inner circle, after the demise of Fouquet. He proved a successful replacement. He enjoyed political and economic freedoms and was free to implement innovations to the economy. Mousnier announced that 'everything connected with finance' was Colbert's 'province- that is, virtually the entire government'- such was Colbert's influence in the daily lives of the French people and government (cf. Mallia-Milanes). As the Intendant of Finances, Colbert ran a tight ship- he was responsible for the group of intendants who were administrators acting as the king's 'eyes and ears' and were in charge of collecting taxes such as the taille (cf. Campbell, Louis xiv, Treasure, Louis xiv) and the Paulette that were due to the royal coffers and Treasury. They were also in charge of 'rooting out corruption'. According to regional studies, each intendant was assigned a province which became his generalite (cf. Campbell, Louis xiv). Colbert ruled the intendants with an iron rod supervising their every move and activities (cf. Treasure, Louis xiv). Whenever the intendants became too powerful, operating beyond their responsibilities- even ultra vires, Colbert would be quick to respond with a reminder that they were answerable to the king and should not in any way, violate their powers. For example, in a letter to de Creil, an intendant to Rouen Colbert alerted de Creil to the limits and boundaries of his powers:

'His Majesty has further ordered me to write you that, in the light of the explanations that you have yourself have provided for each article, he deems you to have been wrong on nearly every count; he has determined that you had set up your own court before which avocats and procureurs appeared along with the parties and that either you yourself or your subdelegates had assumed jurisdiction over cases normally lying within the jurisdiction of the elus and the Cour des Aides. To which he has ordered me to add that, if you do not change your conduct in this regard and adopt a diametrically opposite course of action, he will be unable to retain you in your position' (cf. Louis xiv and France, Mallia- Milanes).

Colbert was a mercantilist implementing protectionist policies which included charging tariffs on foreign items, goods and services in a bid to stimulate and protect domestic producers. As part of his mercantilist policies Colbert sought to realise a balance of trade by exporting 'manufactured goods of high quality' in return for 'gold and silver' (cf. Treasure, Louis xiv). He embarked on major public works and negotiated successfully for the access of the French East India Company to foreign markets, so that they could attain coffee, cotton, dyewoods, fur, pepper and sugar. He founded France's merchant navy and became Secretary of State of the Navy in 1669. As De Wismes noted Colbert created 'a powerful and well-trained navy'. As Mallia-Milanes notes 'oversees trade flourished, colonisation received 'the full backing of the State', industrial development was revitalised and a system of patronage and pensions was introduced' (cf. Mallia-Milanes, Louis xiv and France). Also Colbert encouraged the production of luxury items such as royal tapestry and high quality cloth. A contemporary Ciriacono notes of the silk industry:

'The most important contribution of the Lyons industry lay in the introduction of new motifs and new ways of representing nature. The passion for pomp and splendour flourished under the absolute monarchy, floral motifs were eagerly taken up, with branches and foliages that were larger than life…Lyons, in life, provided an excellent and rewarding meeting place for technical

Louis XIV and Richelieu

and economic development, on one hand, and artistic innovations on the other' (cf. Mallia-Milanes).

As for tapestry, Colbert subsidised and invested some seven million livres for the next twenty years in support of private industries and companies that produced works of art which soon found their way into the great homes- that is to say, the aristocracy and the museums of Europe (cf. Treasure, Louis xiv).

Colbert published around 150 edicts to regulate the guilds and founded several academies which contributed to the intellectual life of France. He also sold offices of the state in order to substantiate the royal coffers as well as dreaming up all kinds of taxes such as the Taille, Paulette and the gabelle (cf. Mansel, King of the World) to pay for the king's domestic and foreign policies. The last point has been disputed by Mallia-Milanes who notes that Colbert was essentially a fiscal conservative 'who reduced expenditure, controlled taxation not to exceed 100 million livres and did his utmost to make the entire fiscal system work uniformly'.

The common view is that the economy during Louis' time was stagnant and experienced weak growth. Campbell disputes such an account- according to Campbell, manufacturing enjoyed a revival where the likes of the cloth industry employed some 1 million people (cf. Campbell, Louis xiv). Colbert was financially and commercially astute. According to Cronin, Colbert carried out a number of reforms to France's economy, raising funds to pay for Louis' projects without necessarily increasing tax. The Taille intake, the chief tax was 'reduced from £14 million in 1661 to an average of £12 million for the years 1662-1682', the majority of Louis' personal rule. Officials were required to 'keep regular accounts', certain taxes were auctioned rather than selling them to a private favoured few, inventories were revised and unauthorised exemptions removed (cf. Cronin, Louis xiv). Tax loopholes and tax avoidances were dealt with. As Cronin notes, Colbert's policies were a success-'excellent results were achieved. In 1661', tax receipts were £26 million, of which £10 million reached the Treasury. Total 'expenditure was £18 million, leaving a deficit of £8 million. [By] 1667, the net receipts had risen to £20 million, while expenditure had fallen to £11 million, leaving a surplus of £9 million' (cf. Cronin, Louis xiv).

As a result of Colbert's economic reforms, France as a whole, flourished- Paris, the capital too.

Colbert's policies can be summed up as 'dirigiste' which is an economic model that supports state intervention in the economy, rather than a laissez faire economy. In other words, Colbert was an ordoliberal anticipating post war Germany and her adoption of said model. As Treasure notes, Colbert had a far more grander and comprehensive concept of gloire than the king. Whereas Louis sought 'la gloire' through his foreign policies, Colbert sought to incarnate the king's 'gloire' in terms of the organisation of the state and its potential to be a powerful organ. For example, Colbert's reforms and codification of the law did much to anticipate the 'later generation's enlightenment'. Colbert also included the arts and the sciences (cf. Treasure, Louis xiv) in his ambitions and plans for the state where he set up institutes that promoted the aforementioned subjects. As well as French artists, Colbert invited men from abroad such as Bernini, the architect of the Vatican to advise on the design of the Louvre, Huygens, 'the astronomer, scientist and inventor of clock' travelled from Holland to France, whilst sculptures were imported from Italy (cf. Ashley, Louis xiv and the Greatness of France). With the support and approval of Louis Colbert created the Petite Academy on 23rd February 1663, consisting of four men of letters, the most notable being Charles Perrault. Louis encouraged the artists in their endeavours: 'You may judge, Messieurs', wrote Louis, 'the esteem which I have for you, because I am entrusting you the thing which is the most precious in the world-my gloire. I am sure you will do marvels; I will try for my part to furnish you with material to be put in hand by men as capable as yourselves'. A further Academy was created out of the Petite (cf. Treasure, Louis xiv). The historian, Peter Robert Campbell has called Colbert one of the 'greatest administrators of the ancient regime' (cf. Campbell, Louis xiv). It is hard not to disagree- Colbert was a highly competent and efficient administrator who diligently worked and came up with several initiatives to improve the economy in a bid to realise the king's 'gloire'.

Michael Le Tellier had been Secretary of State for Military affairs since 1643. He was talent spotted by Mazarin. He is regarded as being an efficient administrator who stayed loyal to Mazarin and the state during the Frondes (cf. Encyclopaedia Britannica, Francois-Michel le Tellier, Marquis de Louvois, Hebermann, Michael le Tellier). In 1677 he was promoted and appointed by Louis to the position of Chancellor of France. He was held in high esteem by the king-'[le Tellier is] both prudent and wise and of modesty which I greatly value[]' (cf. Treasure, Louis xiv). One of his major contributions as secretary of state for the military was to professionalise and improve the once private and disparate army by streamlining the army, bringing it into central control that helped Louis in his foreign adventures (cf. Encyclopaedia Britannica, Treasure, Louis xiv, Wilkinson, Louis xiv). Before Louis and Le Tellier's reforms one could not speak of a 'French army' per se since divisions belonged to disparate owners. Previously the army was scattered all over the place- the subject and property of many private owners. Le Tellier did much to make the army more cohesive and more unified. As Treasure notes, Le Tellier sought to professionalise the army by employing young sound men who were expected to serve for four years and were expected to be single and physically fit- if he 'was destined for the maison du roi he should be a catholic (cf. Treasure, Louis xiv). Le Tellier took a dislike to Protestantism and supported Louis in his endeavours of revoking the Edict of Nantes which had previously granted rights and freedoms to the Huguenot community. Le Tellier purchased the Maquisate from Louvois, handing over the title over to his son Francois-Michel Le Tellier (cf. Cronin, Louis xiv).

Hugues de Lionne was Secretary of State in charge of foreign affairs. After falling out of favour with Richelieu he was restored to such favour under Mazarin. His success include the negation of the Treaty of Aix-la-Chapelle which ended the War of Devolution and the sale of Dunkirk where Charles II of England gave up his sovereign and territorial rights to Dunkirk to his cousin, Louis.

Together these three men- Colbert, Le Tellier and Lionne were soon joined by the Dauphin and the Dauphin's son, all who helped Louis to govern France. After Colbert's departure, his role was filled by Louvois who continued in the same policy trajectory and line of direction consolidating much of Colbert's work (cf.

Cronin, Louis xiv). Louis' team was highly effective, highly competent and highly efficient. Louis enjoyed working with his team. Rather than the nobility, they were drawn from the middle classes who Louis felt were more dispassionate and methodical than those from the passionate nobility. Louis centralised power, but also decentralised that said power where he delegated responsibilities and said power to his ministers of state as well as the intendants who were much closer to the people (cf. Cronin, Louis xiv, Wilkinson, Louis xiv).

According to Cronin, Louis though he seldom read books, soon took an interest in cultivating writers whom he patronised and sponsored. He ordered Chapelain the poet to draw up a list of forty-five French writers and fifteen foreign writers. The list, dated 1664, included, Sainte-Marthe, Moliere, the two Corneilles, Flechier, Racine, Benserade, Quinault and Charles Perrault; Graziani 'well versed in letters and an excellent Italian poet', the historian Conrigius and Johannes Hevelius the astronomer. To these authors, Louis sent a 'gift of gold coins in a silk purse, sometimes amounting to £1,000'. Of course previous leaders had patronised the arts, but none according to Cronin, were so generous and eager in their patronage as Louis was. Louis was always on the lookout for talented writers, not just French, but also international. To Comminges, his agent in England whom he had asked

Louis XIV and Richelieu

for a report on English writers, he noted: 'My intention is to be informed of all that is best and exquisite in all countries and in all branches of knowledge' (cf. Cronin, Louis xiv). Louis' policy on the arts culminated in his appropriation of the Academie Francaise which fell within the sphere of his patronage. He became the 'Protector' of the Academie. The aforementioned writers were supported by the Academie whilst music wise, the likes of composers and musicians such as Jean-Baptiste Lully, Jacques Champion de Chambonnieres, and Francois Couperin thrived. Encouraged by the Academie's success, further academies were opened such as the Academy Royale de Danse in 1661 and in 1669, the Academie d'Opera, which played a part in the development of ballet.

Despite the king's best efforts these academies were a failure, producing only Moliere and Rancine, and even then these two did not compare to the likes of their English counterparts and forebears such as Christopher Marlowe and William Shakespeare.

Louis did not always get his way in matters of policies, proving the view that he was not an absolutist. There were a system of checks and balances where institutions negotiated their respective rights instituting France as fledgling and young democracy. For example, in June 1663, Louis ordered that each province in France should build a hospital to nurse and help the 'sick poor, beggars and orphans'. The parliament of Dijon refused. When Colbert 'proposed a canal between Beaucaire and Aigues-Mortes, the intendant Besons reported: 'The scheme is useful for the service of the King and the good of the provinces, but because of vested interests the States will not pass it; they do not understand the advantages of trade'. Despite these earlier failures, Louis carried out a number of reforms to the parliaments and municipalities which improved the relationship between the king, the centres of government and the localities. According to Cronin 'the new machinery ha[d] begun to work and to work well' (cf. Cronin, Louis xiv).

According to the historian, Albert Sorel Louis was an arbitrary despot who ruled without the support of a constitution:

'It has been widely debated whether France possessed a constitution during the Old Regime. Actually, the most secret archives of the realm might have been searched without discovering its text. The kings did not believe in it, and their jurists denied its existence.

'We should return to the fundamental laws' was the cry in all places whenever the state was troubled and power faltered, but these laws were nowhere to be found. All appealed to them, but no one knew them…It was necessary that the principle of power remain a mystery, and if there was somewhere a fundamental law, it rested

Louis XIV and Richelieu

upon this maxim which eliminated the necessity of establishing others: 'The rights of peoples and those of kings never concur better than in silence' (cf. Church, The Greatness of Louis xiv).

On the contrary. Louis was very much a constitutional and legalistic monarch who did much in his time to improve Frances' legal system, mindful of the constitutional limits to his powers. Louis' reforms were prophetic- his root and branch reforms of the laws anticipated the likes of the Napoleonic code. As Mousnier tells us louis made uses of 'lettres de cachet', the precursor to executive orders by which he informed his ministers and others of his desired policies. With a lettre 'the king arrested, imprisoned, and exiled…When the king himself had spoken, there remained nothing but to submit to his authority, the legal source of justice' (cf. Church, The Greatness of Louis xiv). Louis was highly efficient- he expected and demanded such efficiency from his ministers and of all of those whom he worked with. He was hardworking, diligent and meticulous and 'would spend long hours reading reports and attending councils' (cf. Campbell, Louis xiv). After consultation with his council, Louis issued a set of reforms to update and modernise the legal system. The result was the 'odonnace civile' issued and registered in 1667. Prices for judicial posts were lowered making it more accessible and widening the poole of applicants;

births and marriage had to be registered, legal procedure was made more efficient and was streamlined. Louis in a masterstroke reopened the Paris law school, which had been closed for a hundred years, and opened faculties of law in every French university. In 1670 a code of criminal law was issued. France's legal system improved under Louis and was in robust health. Everyone had access to justice- 'Complaints and petitions', writes Louis, 'arrived in great numbers but I did not allow that to put me off...They enabled me to inform myself in detail about the condition of my people...W[ith] cases of injustice [I] stepped in to rectify them'(cf. Cronin, Louis xiv). Louis was enlightened. He cared deeply for the wellbeing of his people ensuring that they were treated fairly and justly. As Cronin notes, there were two events when Louis decided law-suits against himself- such was the king's desire for fairness and justice (cf. Cronin, Louis xiv). Louis was kind to a fault. In 1685, he published his 'Code Noir' which sought to improve the wellbeing of slaves in the West Indies. According to the terms of the Code- slaves had the option of being baptised- if they wished and could rest on Sundays and holidays. They were allowed to marry. Masters who abused their position where liable for punishment. Emancipation was made easier to achieve. As Cronin notes '[t]he code was an outstanding humanitarian measure far in advance of its time' (cf. Cronin, Louis xiv).

Louis XIV and Richelieu

As Hassall notes, personally, Louis was kind, well mannered, polite and self-composed. He was sober, 'self controlled', 'rarely laughed' and was recollected, 'seldom giving way to anger'. According to Saint-Simon, 'He would have been every inch the king...even if he had been born under the roof of a beggar'. This is supported by Bolingbroke who declared that 'if he was not the greatest king he was the best actor of majesty, at least, that ever filled a throne' (cf. Hassall, Louis xiv). Louis had a conscience. As Cronin notes, a sizeable part of the funds raised by Colbert were used for improving the welfare and wellbeing of the poor (cf. Cronin, Louis xiv). In that sense Louis was enlightened and well meaning.

According to Saint-Simon Louis' passion for grandeur and authority 'smothered all other considerations within him' (cf. Mallia-Milanes, Louis xiv and France). I do not accept this view. Louis' time in office was filled with many activities designed to bring glory to France. The King was diligent involving himself in the political, social, economic and cultural lives of his people. Louis did much to improve France as a functioning democracy, society and country. The next three chapters deal with Louis and his quest to ensure his 'gloire' for all posterity.

CHAPTER 4

Louis at Versailles

At the instigation of Louis, his central power base and nerve centre became the palace of Versailles, out in the country and away from the hustle and bussle of Parisian city life where he governed France in concert with his ministers. As a result of Colbert's successful financial policies, Louis indulged himself in creating the lavish and grand palace at Versailles funded by Colbert (cf. Cronin, Louis xiv). The two- Colbert and Louis clashed over Versailles- Colbert wanted Louis to concentrate on the Louvre, in Paris which 'would bring him glory' rather than Versailles which was only a place of 'pleasure and diversion' yet the king in the end was granted his wish to settle at Versailles. Louis was diligent in saving funds for the construction of the palace (cf. Cronin, Louis xiv). As Bossuet notes, Versailles was built in order 'to make the people respect him' and acted as a permanent sand constant reminder of Louis's gloire (cf. Treasure, Louis xiv). Versailles was to be the King's centre of government. The palace stood as a model to other European powers and monarchs who followed suit and built their own courts and centres of government just like Versailles. For example, Treasure tells us that '[t]he [Holy Roman] Emperor Leopold built Schonbrunn in imitation [of Versailles], [whilst] scores of German princelings planted out miniature [palaces just like] Versailles [in order] to impress their authority on their subjects' (cf. Treasure, Louis xiv)- such was the significance, importance and substantiveness of Versailles and all that she entailed.

According to Cronin, the idea of Versailles came in the summer of 1661, the year of the beginning of his personal rule. Louis preferred the country to the busy city (cf. Cronin, Louis xiv). Another view is that Louis created Versailles where he required the presence and attendance of the nobles so that he could keep tabs on the nobility and ensure that another revolt and frondes would never ever occur again. As Saint-Simon notes Louis had 'the credible advantage' of Versailles being set in a single residence outside of Paris due to the fact that Versailles 'imposed orderliness on everybody and secured dispatch and facility to his affairs' (cf. Treasure, Louis xiv). Another view is that the nobility were kept at court- not so much to 'render

Louis XIV and Richelieu

them powerless' but so that they could collaborate with the king for the greater good and glory of France where in a grand coalition- the crown, nobility and church would govern in the supreme interest of France. The latter view is more credible and plausible. On 6th May 1682, Louis took possession of his new palace. Work on the palace had been substantially completed (cf. Cronin, Louis xiv).

Versailles was very much the pet project of Louis. As Treasure notes Louis took a keen interest in the art and architecture of the new palace, often collaborating and instructing those responsible for designing and building the palace such as Le Vau, the chief architect, his successor, Jules Hardounin-Mansart, Charles le Brun, the king's chief painter and Le Notre, the royal gardener (cf. Campbell, Louis xiv, Mitford, The Sun King, Cronin, Louis xiv, Treasure, Louis xiv) offering his own views and opinions in the process as to the style and makeup of Versailles. It took Versailles, from a small hunting lodge to the sprawling and opulent palace it is today to be completed from 1661 to 1669 and took 25,000 workers per day before it was complete (cf. Campbell, Louis xiv).

The palace was to be different from the stuffy and gloomy Saint Germain and the Louvre where it would be light and airy with large windows to let the light in and extensive gardens suitable for short and long walks outside. Versailles would be both a home for the royal family and the working base for the nobility- in short- 'the centre of government' where Louis would rule his kingdom in coalition and collaboration with his ministers (cf. Cronin, Louis xiv). In a sense Versailles was France's glory incarnate and hence it was to be both large and impressive (cf. Cronin, Louis xiv)- even forbidding. Not only was Versailles created for France it was designed to inspire respect and to demonstrate Louis' and France's greatness and glory to the world (cf. Mansel, King of the World: The Life of Louis xiv).

Versailles was built with 'precious materials, inlaid coloured marble, the contrast of dark tones and gilded brass, sculpture, medallions and reminiscences of Rome. In the King's five state apartments the walls were of marble, inlaid in geometrical patterns; marble, too, were the walls of the grand gallery, or Galerie des Glaces, eighty yards long and occupying almost the entire façade of the central section on the west side. Seventeen high windows curtained with white damask looked out on the gardens and were reflected in seventeen arched mirrors lining the opposite wall...The ornaments, here as throughout Versailles, were decorated with laurels, lyres, sunflowers, radiant crowns and all the classical attributes of the sun. The ceiling, the work of Le Brun from 1679 to 1682, comprised thirty paintings of evens, chiefly victories, in Louis's reign' (cf. Cronin, Louis xiv).

Louis XIV and Richelieu

Versailles was opulent. It was populated with the 'statues of the gods and goddesses of classical antiquity, with statues of Venus, Diana, Ceres, Galatea, Proserpine, Latona, Aurora and Amphitre, of Jupiter, Apollo, Neptune, Bacchus, Saturn, Proteus and Zephyr, of nymphs and Tritons, Vestals, cupids and fauns'. Versailles had extensive gardens. As Louis notes in his short 'Guide to the Gardens of Versailles'- 'we go to the Pyramid, where we pause a moment, then return to the chateau by the marble stairway between the 'Ecorcheur' and the 'Venus honteuse'. At the top off the steps we turn to look at the flower-beds to the north, the statues, vases, crowns, the Pyramid and what can be seen of Neptune…'. There was a 'mile long…grand canal [which was] gilded [with] a hundred swans from Denmark, two little yachts from England, carved and gilded galleys decked with a red and white streamers…fringed with gold, a small warship and a fleet of gondolas, manned in by fourteen Venetian gondoliers' (cf. Cronin, Louis xiv).

According to the historian, Nancy Mitford, on 6 May 1682, Louis made the announcement that Versailles was to be his central home and central locality of his government. He set off to Versailles 'accompanied by his family, his ministers and the whole Court' (cf. Mitford, The Sun King).

As Wilkinson, notes Louis 'dominated' the court

which he enjoyed. He was 'charm[ing] and had good sense'. As Robert Briggs has noted '[t]he evidence suggests to me that he was often rather good at handling people, he had a real grasp of psychology and usually behaved very decently in human terms' (cf. Wilkinson, Louis xiv). Despite the false start that occurred between louis and the nobility during the frondes- all was forgiven by Louis- there were no residue of hard feelings. He enjoyed the presence of the nobles at court and encouraged their attendance to court- 'we never see him'- that was Louis' light hearted comment at those who members of the nobility who failed to appear at court. All nobles were very much desired and their presence was very much required (cf. Wilkinson, Louis xiv).

Life at Versailles was filled with ritual and spectacle much of it- if not all centred upon the king with the king at the centre where all gravitated to 'the roi-soleil'-the sun king.

Louis had a daily routine which he stuck to. As Cronin tells us:

'The King usually awoke at the time he had named the evening before, but if not, when the palace clock began to chime eight, the first valet de chambre approached the king's bed. 'Sire, it is sticking eight'. As soon as the King was fully awake, his brother and his sons were allowed to enter and speak to him. At quarter past eight the wet-nurse who had suckled the king in his infancy came in and kissed him...

He put on his slippers and a dressing gown passed outside the balustrade and seated himself in an elbow chair. Every other morning he shaved. 'He often spoke of hunting, and sometimes said a word to somebody. No toilet table was near to him; he simply had a mirror held before him'. He then put his wig and signified that the grand lever might begin.

The hundred or so courtiers who had the privilege of attending the grand lever were now admitted to see the king dress...Still in his dressing gown, the King hen ate breakfast from a service of porcelain and gold. It was a very light meal of white bread, wine and water-Louis never touched tea, coffee or chocolate.

...The lever ended when the King passed into his study. Here he issued orders for the day and gave audiences, before attending Mass in the palace chapel. During Mass he said his rosary: he had inherited it from Henri IV... After Mass he held a Council in his study, except on Thursday, when he gave audiences, and on Friday when he talked to his confessor.

Dinner was served at one o'clock. Like all the King's meals it was prepared in the kitchens of the Grand Commun, a large square building opposite the south wing, where 1,500 servants and gentlemen servants lodged...

(Versailles had its own shopping centre)

The King dined alone. His dinner was usually of three courses, with dessert…

After lunch the King spent a little time giving biscuits to his setter and pointers, of which he was very fond…The afternoon was spent either stag-hunting, shooting on foot or walking in his gardens for exercise and in order to see his workmen. During his walks, all of the courtiers might follow the king. On his return he worked for an hour or more in his study…

The main meal of the day was served at ten o'clock in the first ante-room. It was always on a grand scale: the royal family at table, and many courtiers and ladies present, seated or standing…

After supper there was usually some amusement such as a ball, a concert, card games or, if the weather was fine, a fete in the gardens. Otherwise the King spent about an hour talking with the royal family in one of his smaller private rooms. At the end of his day he passed into his bedroom for the ceremony of the coucher…The King named the hour at which he wished to be awakened and told the Grand Master of the Wardrobe what dress he would wear on the following day. Then all withdrew except the first valet chambre and garcons…the King then went to bed' (cf. Cronin, Louis xiv, see Mallia-Milanes,

Louis XIV and Richelieu

Louis xiv and France for an another summary of the king's daily ritual at Versailles).

As Cronin notes, Louis had always lived in public-something that he did not seem to mind. Louis was 'sociable and enjoyed having people around him'. Louis's presence amongst his courtiers and the daily ritual at Versailles was necessary for his 'gloire' signifying his importance (cf. Cronin, Louis xiv). According to Wilkinson, both courtiers and members of the government lived side by side, competing with each other for attention of the king who exercised and maintained full control (cf. Wilkinson, Louis xiv).

The historian, R. Lockyer notes that Versailles:

'was more than a folly, more than a preposterous and extravagant display of personal glory. It was consciously designed to dazzle Europe and to tame the French aristocracy. As such it succeeded, beyond doubt. At the same time, it cut off the leaders of French society, including the king himself, from the people they ruled. The court…bore little relation to the world of ordinary men and women except in so far as they were taxed…to maintain it. All this glory was built on the backs of the peasants, and no account of Louis [xiv]'s achievement would be complete that put in Versailles but left out this other France in which incessant toil, poverty and starvation were daily realities' (cf. Mallia-Milanes, Louis xiv and France).

Far from Louis being aloof from his subjects cocooned as he was by being surrounded with his ministers and the nobility, Lockyer supported by Levron tells us that louis was 'accessible' to the rest of the general public. 'Anyone was free to enter the palace'. In 1682, inscribed on a celebratory and ceremonial coin minted for the glory of Versailles- a maxim on it read-'the apartments opened to the public. Kindness and Magnificence of the Princes'. All were welcomed to Versailles and all were greeted and received with the good tidings of the king and queen. The king was open to any person who had a 'valid reason for seeing him in an audience' (cf. Hatton, Louis xiv and Absolutism). As Levron notes, women were expected to be in court dress accompanied with an escort whilst men were required to have a sword- once these conditions were satisfied then all were accepted and all welcomed (cf. Hatton, Louis xiv and Absolutism). Louis made himself open to all those who wanted to see the king. As well as the conduct of affairs of state, Versailles too was filled with balls and fettes designed to celebrate, illustrate and demonstrate the king's 'gloire'.

As one visitor Madam de Sevigne relayed to Madam de Grignan:

'I was on Saturday at Versailles with the Villars…[T]

hate fine apartment of the kings…is furnished with the utmost magnificence;…[the people] pass from one room to another without being crowded…The Queen talked to me of my illness, nor did she leave you unmentioned' (cf. Mallia-Milanes, Louis xiv and France)

The Dutch historian Jeroen Duindam has questioned the effectiveness of Louis' powers which he exercised at court, calling such thoughts as myth:

'As an instrument of power, the myth Louis xiv helped to create was just as important as the standing army he greatly expanded at the same time. The myth, however, retained its effectiveness much longer, for down to the present day Louis' power continues to be overestimated' (cf. Wilkinson, Louis xiv).

I disagree- Louis right from the beginning of his residence at Versailles, till the very end maintained order at court which he used as his base in coalition with members of government and members of the nobility. He retained his powers from beginning to the end. Versailles and all she entails remains one of the best creations and inventions of Louis' reign. Versailles was busy with activity- there was 'study work: reports, dispatches, correspondence, and interviews with prospective generals'. Court life went on, even if it was different from the heydays of joviality during the 1660s and 1670s. All were sober, present and correct, now that Mme de Maintenon, the king's second wife who was a devout catholic was at court in coalition with her 'reformed husband'- any acts of sexual licence or drunkenness was 'kept behind closed doors' and in private. However, there were services performed in the palace chapel, large meals were still being consumed by the king, 'concerts, receptions, parades were uninterrupted despite the war' (cf. Wilkinson, Louis xiv). Louis through his personality and wits controlled and dominated France.

Versailles was a popular and busy court filled with ministers, politicians, members of the nobility and members of the church. La Bruryere in 'De la Cour' notes:

'The great persons of the nation assemble every day, a certain hour, in a temple which they call a church. At the far end of this temple stands an altar consecrated to their god, where a priest celebrates the mysteries which they call holy, sacred and redoutable. The great ones form an enormous circle at the foot of this alter, and, standing erect, they turn their baks directly to the priest and the holy mysteries and lift their faces towards the king, who is seen kneeling in a galley, and upon whom they appear to be focusing their whole heart and spirit. One cannot avoid seeing in this custom a kind of subordination; for the people appear to be worshipping their prince, while the prince [in turn] worships God' (cf. Mallia-Milanes, Louis xiv and France).

According to Louis' contemporary Saint-Simon,

Versailles consumed the king and his preoccupations leaving little else for his attention on both domestic and foreign policies. According to this view Louis lost the plot being distracted by events at Versailles:

'Who could count [Louis xiv's] buildings? At the same time, who would not deplore the pride, the capriciousness and the bad taste so evident in them? He abandoned Saint-German and built nothing ornamental or convenient in Paris except Port Royal, and this out of sheer necessity. Paris is inferior to many cities all over Europe…He abandoned [Saint-Germain]…for Versailles, the dullest and most unworthy of places, without views, woods, water or soil as everywhere around is shifting sand or swamp' (cf. Mallia-Milanes, Louis xiv and France).

That is not strictly true. I disagree with Saint-Simon's analysis. As Wilkinson notes, Louis 'built palaces in the vicinity of Versailles [such as] Trianon and Clagny' as well as Marly (cf. Wilkinson, Louis xiv). Though I agree that Paris and Saint-Germain were not- as it were the primary concerns of Louis, he delegated such responsibilities of the wellbeing of these two cities as well as others to the care of his chief intendant Colbert. Paris was not neglected: as one Englishman commented 'I view the city [of Paris] in all its parts…I must needs confess it to be one of the most beautiful and magnificent in Europe, and in which a traveller might find novelties enough for six months for daily entertainments' (cf. Mallia-Milanes, Louis xiv and France). With Versailles as his power base Louis was interested in all manners of issues concerning France- all received his attention.

CHAPTER 5

Louis and Religion

As Cronin notes, religion in Louis' times played a prominent and significant part in the lives of his people. As a devout Roman Catholic, Louis sought to confirm and conform all within his country to the dictats of his religion. Louis took his titles as the 'Most Christian King' and 'Eldest Son of the Church' bestowed on him by the papacy seriously and took up the catholic clause with much relish and much sincerity (cf. Wilkinson, Louis xiv, Cronin, Louis xiv). As Wilkinson notes, Louis was guided by the principle of 'One God, One Faith, One Law'. Everyone in his kingdom was to subscribe to the king's religion of Roman Catholicism (cf. Wilkinson, Louis xiv, Wolf, Louis xiv).

During Louis' times, as Cronin, notes, new orders sprang up and 'flourished: Mere du Calvaire's Clairettes,

Marcelle Germaine's Daughters of Providence, Venerable Francoise de la Croix's nursing sisters. Jean Jacques Olier founded the Sulpicians to train priests, and the Duke de Ventadour the Company of the Blessed Sacrament, a secret group of laymen to guard public morals (It was they who had 'Tartuffe' banned) (cf. Cronin, Louis xiv).

Louis' rule in France witnessed the success of Roman Catholic scholars and divines such as Blaise Pascal who wrote the famous 'Pensees' which contains in albeit an unorthodox fashion, proofs for the existence of god, Francois Fenelon who was a tutor to the Dauphin's eldest son, the seven year old Duke of Burgundy and was in his own right, a talented theologian and writer as well as Madame du Guyon, noted for her eccentricities in matters of religion (cf. Mitford, The Sun King, Cronin, Louis xiv) .

Louis was faced with much dissent both from within the catholic church as well as those who were outside the church. As Wilkinson notes, Louis clashed with 'the Papacy, the Gallicans, the Huguenots, the Jansenists, the Pietists' as well as the Quietists (cf. Wilkinson, Louis xiv).

Louis's father, Louis xiii enacted the Edict of Nantes which had granted the French protestant Huguenots the right to practice their religion freely and without interference from any one or any institution. As Wilkinson notes, 'Louis did not like the Huguenots'. Louis explained his policy concerning the Huguenots:

'I believed, my son, that the best means to reduce gradually the number of Huguenots in my kingdom was, in the first place, not to press them at all by any new rigour against them, to implement what they had obtained from my predecessors but to grant them nothing further. I carefully put a stop everywhere to the schemes of these religionists, as in the Faubourg Saint-Germain, where I learned that they were beginning to conduct secret meetings and schools of their sect. But as to the favours that depended solely on me, I resolved not to grant them any, and this out of kindness rather than out of bitterness, so as to oblige them to consider if they had some good reason for depriving themselves voluntarily of the advantages which they could share with all my other subjects. But I am still a long way, my son, from having exhausted every thing that I have in mind for recalling peacefully those whom birth, education and most often a zeal without knowledge hold in good faith to these pernicious errors' (cf. Wilkinson, Louis xiv).

Louis dispatched with his earlier intentions not to grant further rights to the Huguenots and sought to abolish all such rights. According to Wilkinson, Louis could not see the point of the further existence of the Huguenots since the church had recovered, had overcome and had dealt with the very corrupt practices that the Huguenots had attacked hence Louis could see no point in their raison d'etre and further existence. That is one interpretation. Another view, according to the historian, Phillip Mansel is that as well as internal forces which drove Louis to revoke the Edict, Louis embarked on said revocation in order consolidate his role as leader of Catholic Europe in a bid to outwit his rival, the Catholic House of Austria (cf. Mansel, King of the World: The Life of Louis xiv). Despite the Huguenots loyalty to the king when he was Dauphin during the frondes, Louis in a most ungracious and ungrateful manner revoked the rights of the Huguenots to freely practice their religion by enacting the 'Edict of Fontainebleau' on Thursday 22 October, 1685 (cf. Wilkinson, Louis xiv). The Edict of Fontainebleau revoked the 'Edict of Nantes' and disapplied the rights of the Huguenots to practice their religion. Part of the Edict reads as follows:

'The best and greater part of our subjects of the R.P.R. [religion pretendue reforme] have embraced the Catholic faith; and as by reason of this the Edict of Nantes useless, we have judged that we cannot do better, to efface entirely the memory of the troubles, the confusion, and the evils that the progress of the false religion have caused in our realm than to revoke entirely the above edict' (cf. Wilkinson, Louis xiv).

All Huguenots were expected to convert to Roman Catholicism and Huguenot ministers were given two weeks to convert or else leave France. The Revocation enacted the closure of protestant churches and called for the cessation of services, protestant schools were closed and all those born to protestant families should undergo conversion and be baptised as Catholics (cf. Wilkinson, Louis xiv). Protestant pastors were prevented from administering to the sick in hospitals and were banned from teaching in schools (cf. Campbell, Louis xiv). Some 200,000 Huguenots left the country seeking refuge and safety in 'Brandenburg, Prussia, England, Holland, Switzerland and the New World'. Many were highly skilled and arguably did some damage to the operation of the French economy since the country suffered from brain flight (cf. Wilkinson, Louis xiv). As one diarist notes:

'The French persecution of the Protestants, raging with utmost barbarity, exceeding what the very heathens used: Innumerable persons of the greater birth, & riches, leaving all their earthly substance & hardly escaping with their lives, dispers'd thro' all the Countries of Europe: The French Tyrant, abrogating the Edict of Nantes &c in favour of them, & without any Cause on the suddaine, demolishing all their Churches, banishing, Imprisoning, sending to the Gallies all the Ministers' (cf. Mallia-Milanes, Louis xiv and France).

One cannot see the point of Louis's policies concerning the Huguenots. Though Louis's inner circle and court approved of Louis's actions (cf. Ashley, Louis xiv and the Greatness of France), many of Louis' fellow Catholic bishops did not support Louis' revocation of Nantes- and neither for that matter- the Pope who pointed out that 'Christ did not use armed forces to further the Gospel'. On the issue of the Huguenot problem, Louis found himself isolated with little support for his polices (cf. Wilkinson, Louis xiv). It is hard not to disagree with the French historian, Roland Mousnier's summary:

'The methods he used were inhuman, an affront to the dignity of the man, an contrary to the spirt of Christianity, whilst forced communion was a sin against the Holy Ghost. In this respect Louis was indeed a tyrant' (cf. Wilkinson, Louis xiv).

Another problem within Louis' kingdom was the presence of Jansenism. Jansenists were on the puritanical wing of the catholic church where they stressed the existence of 'original sin', 'human depravity' and the 'necessity of grace' in their theology and account of human nature. According to the movement which drew inspiration from the writings of Cornelius Jansen human works are not necessary in an account of salvation- only gods grace will do and is sufficient. Louis disliked this sect within the church and did much to quell them down. In his Memoirs Louis notes the movement as one 'which teaches that knowledge is not necessary in order for a man to be saved' hence rejecting the absolutist-as it were account of pure grace as the saving constitute of human nature. Louis disliked the movement's puritanism which jarred with his moderate, sensible, gentle and hopeful Christianity informed by the likes of the gentle spirituality of Saint Francis de Sales (cf. de Sales, An Introduction to the Devout Life). At the end of 1660, Louis told his bishops that he had 'resolved' to outlaw 'the pernicious sect [which] should be utterly rooted out' (cf. Cronin, Louis xiv). Historians such as Wilkinson have noted that Louis 'made a problem out of a non-problem'. The relatively small number of Jansenists did not pose a political threat. According to Wilkinson, 'Louis [] gave them significance by persecuting them'. One could argue in favour of Louis' policy in the sense that the Jansenist movement was heretical and an affront to catholic teaching. Rome supported Louis' and the Jesuits' opposition to the movement by the publication of Pope Pius x's 'Unigenitus De Fili' which outlawed the movement.

Meanwhile, there was a dispute over the 'regale' which was income taken by Louis over vacant bishophoric seats. However the regale was not extended to new territories conquered by France since 1274, such as Brittany and

Languedoc. In order to fund the Dutch wars which was proving expensive, Louis in a bid to make up the financial shortfall, extended the regale to the 'whole of France'. Louis faced opposition from two bishops- 'Pavillon of Alet and Caulet of Pamiers who refused to acknowledge [the king's] claim'. Louis appealed to Rome but the new Pope Innocent xi was unsympathetic to Louis' predicament and 'threatened Louis with excommunication'. Louis in retaliation convened a council of bishops (cf. Wilkinson, Louis xiv, Campbell, Louis xiv) to deal with the domestic woes of the king and his relationship with Rome and provide a solution and way out of the diplomatic mess. As Wilkinson notes the Four Gallican Articles and the Gallican church emerged out of the council and was a direct response to the problems of the regale (cf. Wilkinson, Louis xiv, Campbell, Louis xiv).

According to the Gallican Articles published on the 19 March 1682, under the direction of Bossuet:

(1) That the Pope has no authority over the temporal power
(2) That the spiritual authority of the Popes should be regulated by General Councils
(3) That the exercise of Papal authority should be in accordance with the usages of the Gallican Church; and

(4) Papal decisions in matters of faith are not valid till they have received the consent of the church' (cf. Hassall, Louis xiv)

According to Wilkinson, the Council sought to stress the independence of the French catholic church from Rome, 'the independence of the crown, the superiority of councils to the pope…and the indisputable authority of French law' (cf. Wilkinson, Louis xiv). Out of the council emerged the Gallican church, which though catholic, was independent of Rome.

The French bishops sought to appeal to the totality of the king and the in his dealing with temporal matters where he was not bound by dictats from Rome concerning his jurisdiction in the temporal sphere. In a sense the Gallican church was a temporal cousin of the Anglican church in a sense that it downplayed the Papacy's influence over the domestic church yet differed from said Anglicanism in the sense that it still acknowledges the papacy's role in some matters over the national church, particularly concerning its influence in the spiritual sphere. Relations improved when Innocent's successor assented to the papal thrown who was more accommodating of Louis' needs. In reply, Louis discontinued the Gallican movement (cf. Wilkinson, Louis xiv).

The final opposition that Louis faced was the quietist

movement, which was a faction within the catholic church. The foundations of the movement can be found in the writings of a certain Madam de Guyon. Her writings stressed the passive awareness of the divine nullifying the need for active works- its rejection of active works in a sense was a repetition of the jansenist movement that had earlier attracted the ire of Louis. Guyon came to the attention of Louis wife, Madam de Maintenon in 1688 who was so impressed with Guyon that she invited Guyon to give a lecture at Saint-Cyr, a school for girls cofounded by the king and his wife. However once Maintenon was alerted to the heterodox nature of quietism by her confessor, probably due to the movement's rejection of active works and its support of passiveness Maintenon self-corrected and banned all talk of the movement. Guyon had fallen out of favour. Soon, the tutor to the Dauphin's son, Francois Fenelon, came to the defence of Madam de Guyon in his 'Explication' where he noted that there are moments in the life of the church when it is challenged by prophets who scandalises the church but in time becomes accepted as prophetic where such mystics are validated and contribute much to the wellbeing of the church. Louis was annoyed by Fenelon's defence- 'He has the most fanciful mind of any man in my kingdom'. Meanwhile Fenelon's defence attracted the attention and anger of Jacques-Benigne Bossuet who attacked the substance of Fenelon's defence of quietism. After two years, Rome condemned Fenelon's book (cf. Cronin, Louis xiv, Mitford, The Sun King).

According to Cronin, all of the religious events deeply influenced the king who now decided to focus less on the externals and rituals of religion. Instead he focused on agents such as love and compassion which could be just a valuable as 'knowledge, work and achievement'. Accordingly, the very movements such as Jansenism and Quietism that Louis sought to quell influenced the king – even more than he cared to consciously admit. As Cronin notes, 'the principles of humility and submissive love of God's will [associated with the two aforementioned movements] had not been crushed, only driven underground'. These events would impact on the later years of Louis reign (cf. Cronin, Louis xiv).

CHAPTER 6

Foreign Policy

'You are destined to command the entire universe'- that was Jean-Baptiste Tavernier's comment to Louis in 1676 (cf. Mansel, King of the World: The Life of Louis xiv). Inspired by this comment, Louis embarked on foreign adventures designed to increase and substantiate France's empire in a bid to incarnate and realise his 'gloire'. As Mansel notes, Louis was a global player and turned France into a global power setting up colonies in America, Africa and India and sent 'missionaries and mathematicians to the Emperor of China' (cf. Mansel, King of the World: The Life of Louis xiv) in addition to the five wars that Louis embarked on. In other words- Louis increased the global presence and global influence that France enjoyed.

During Louis's rule over France he embarked on a total of five wars designed to help him realise the account of 'gloire'- that is to say 'glory' which was to be realised in his reign. The wars included, the Franco-Dutch war, the War of the League of Augsburg, the War of Spanish Succession and two shorter wars- the War of Devolution and the War of the Reunions.

According to Louis at age thirty, he noted that 'My dominant passion is certainly love of Glory'. And so was the trajectory and direction of rule of Louis marked out and given in coherent form the idea and concept of 'gloire'. Louis was introduced to the concept and principle right back from his childhood. It was in his 'history books, in poems, in the plays of Corneille, in ballets, in opera, he had heard the word 'gloire' ring like an exclamation of awe…The great Kings, Charlemagne and Henri IV, were remembered from their glorious military exploits; so too the Roman Emperors, always hovering in the background of the seventeenth-century imagination: Julius Caesar, Augustus, Trajan' (cf. Cronin, Louis xiv). As well as his domestic policies he sought to achieve 'gloire' from his foreign adventures and escapades.

Louis' first war was the War of Devolutions in 1667 to 1688. France occupied large parts of the Spanish Netherlands and Franche-Comte, both provinces of Spain. Louis sought to justify the war on the basis that these territories had "devolved' to him by right of his marriage to the Spanish Infanta Maria Theresa. Results of the war were mixed- 'France withdrew from Franche -Comte and the Spanish Netherlands' but she retained 'eleven towns and their surrounding areas' (cf. Macintosh, 1973).

Louis' second war was the Franco-Dutch war which began in 1672. As Cronin notes, Louis disliked Holland for a number of reasons which led to his declaration of war on Dutch territories. First, Holland was a protestant and Calvanist republic which discriminated against Roman Catholics- this was at odds with Louis, a Catholic monarch (cf. Cronin, Louis xiv, Dunlop, Louis xiv). Second Holland was a barrier to Louis' territorial claims- for example she had prevented Louis' 'complete annexation of the Spanish Netherlands'. Third, 'Holland was a centre of political opposition and anti-monarchism'- the Dutch media published attacks on the French King and his mistresses- something which deeply annoyed Louis. Finally, the most important reason for Louis' dislike of Holland was her economic success in the world of commerce and finance- the Dutch 'per head were richer than the French and becoming steadily richer'. After a trade dispute when the dutch enforced a trade barrier and embargo against French wine and brandy (cf. Cronin, Louis xiv), Louis took matters into his own hands and declared war on Holland in order to protect France's commercial and economic interests. On 6 April 1672, Louis ordered his army to invade the United Provinces. 'I have decided',

Louis announced, 'that it is more advantageous and more to my glory to attack four places on the Rhine simultaneously and to command in person at all four. I have chosen Rheinberg, Wesel, Burick and Orsoy'. The war was off to a bright start- Louis captured all four territories. The war concluded with a 'special commercial treaty between France and Holland, whereby the more liberal 1664 tariff replaced that of 1667. According to Louis, 'I was resolved to make peace…but I wished to conclude it gloriously for me and advantageously for my kingdom. I wished to reimburse myself by the rights of conquest…and to console myself thus for the end of war that I had fought for both pleasure and success' (cf. Wolf, Louis xiv). Louis then signed separate treaties with other countries that we involved in the war'. By the Treaty of Westphalia, France [] received the land-graviate of Upper and Lower Alsace in full sovereignty, and the 'provincial prefecture' of ten Alsatian cities, the most important of which were Colmer, Landau and Munster'. According to Cronin, the second war, in what was a remarkable turnaround, granted Louis 'success' and 'military glory' (cf. Cronin, Louis xiv). Peter Robert Campbell disagrees- 'the war seems to have been the most serious of his reign' According to Fenelon:

'So many troubles have been devastating all of Europe for more than twenty years, so much blood split, so many outrages committed, so many provinces pillaged, so many towns and villages reduced to ashes, are the disastrous consequences of the war of 1672, started for your gloire and so as to humiliate those makers of gazettes and medals in Holland. That war is still the true source of all the evils that France is suffering from. Since that war you have always wanted to grant peace as a master, and impose the terms, instead of offering them with justice and moderation. That is why peace could not last'.

I do not agree with Campbell's or Fenelon's assessments. Louis succeeded in negotiating a better trade deal and gained many territories. As a result Louis had brought honour and pride back to the burgeoning French empire.

The third war was the War of the Reunions which began in 1683. The war was a further sequel to the War of Devolutions and the Franco-Dutch war. Louis sought to consolidate the 'defensible boundaries along France's northern and eastern borders'. Despite the Treaty of Nijmegen, Louis ignored the treaty and in 1681 his troops annexed Strasbourg and in 1682 occupied the Principality of Orange, then a possession of William of Orange'. French support for the Turks in their war with Austria, allowed Louis to 'capture Strasbourg and Luxembourg [plus Louis] consolidate[d] his position in Alsace. The

Truce of Ratisbon concluded the war. It was the high point of France's territorial gains.

The fourth war began in 1688. It is known as the War of Augsburg- also known as the Nine Years' War. It was a conflict between France and a European coalition composed of the 'Holy Roman Empire(led by Louis' in-laws, the Hapsburgs), the Dutch republic, England, Spain, Savoy and Portugal'. The conflict was fought in Europe as well as North America and India. Louis sought to seek territory that was consistent with his dynastic claims. The resulting Treaty of Ryswick, allowed Louis to keep 'the whole of Alsace', including Strasbourg. Lorraine was returned to the Duke but Louis reserved the right for his troops to march through the territory. Louis gave up gains on the right of the Rhine. New French fortresses were abolished. Within three years Charles II of Spain would pass away, plunging Europe in Louis' fifth and final war- the War of the Spanish Succession.

After Charles II's vacancy of the Spanish throne which he left behind without a successor a debate ensued over who would govern Spain., The French Bourbons and the Spanish Hapsburgs both had claims to the Spanish throne. Through Louis' marriage to the Spanish Infanta Maria Theresa Louis he sought to make a claim through his wife's Spanish heritage to the Spanish throne, given that she was the eldest daughter of Phillip iv of Spain (cf.

Louis XIV and Richelieu

Treasure, Louis xiv), Hassall, Louis xiv). Louis also had a claim on behalf of his son Phillip whose mother, Maria Theresa was a Spanish Hapsburg who was the eldest daughter of Philip iv of Spain (the father of Charles II) (cf. Hassall, Louis XIV, Ashley, Louis xiv and the Greatness of France). According to Louis, Maria Theresa's renunciation of the Spanish throne was void and nullified since the Cortes and the Parliaments of Paris had ever approved and 'ratified the renunciation (cf. Hassall, Louis xiv). Louis himself also had claims in his own right since his mother Anne of Austria was a Spanish Hapsburg. Through his son, mother and wife Louis thus had a triple claim to the Spanish throne. Louis own personal claim to the Spanish throne- (he was half French and half Spanish) seems to have eluded the king. Louis had a quartet of claims to Spain- as father, grandfather, son and husband- all tied up with Spain. After the treaty of partition between Louis and William III of England to partition Spain, giving territory to France (cf. Mansell, King of the World), this was rejected by the Spanish. Instead Charles named Phillip of Anjou, Louis's second grandson (cf. Mansell, King of the World) as heir presumptive. If Anjou refused then the throne would be offered to Archduke Charles, younger son of Leopold I, Holy Roman Emperor. Phillip was proclaimed king starting a war between France and Spain on one hand and Grand Alliance of European allies on the other. According to the Alliance France had too much power with the Bourbon's control of both France and Spain which were the major spheres and centres of power in Europe. The Alliance sought to avoid a monopoly of French Bourbon power in Spain and France in mind that there should ideally be a balance of power. After the war, Phillip's position as king of Spain was consolidated- albeit with the proviso that he renounced all personal rights he had or his descendants had in their claims to the French throne, thus allaying the Alliance's fears. The battle left France in a powerful position where she ascended to the heights of being a global power and a global influence. The battle is now known as the War of the Spanish Succession.

CONCLUDING THOUGHTS

According to the liberal historian, G P Gooch, 'the principal legacy of Louis xiv was a powerful and centralised France' (cf. Church, Louis xiv and the Greatness of France). I disagree. The principal legacy of Louis was the realisation of France as a powerful and dominate European democracy and nation state where France gained a self identity and self confidence that had previously eluded her. Far from being centralised, France enjoyed through Louis' devolvement and decentralisation a series of institutions that made France a modern, successful, bureaucratic and administrative state. All in Louis' kingdom enjoyed responsibilities and freedoms contributing to the common and public good of France.

As Goubert astutely notes, Louis and his colleagues 'left behind them a France that was territorially larger, militarily better defended, with a more effective administration and to a large extent pacified' (cf. Church, The Greatness of Louis xiv).

Louis left behind a France that had several flourishing institutions such as a constitutional monarchy, a team of talented government ministers who enjoyed freedoms in their respective briefs, an advanced and complex system of councils, a legal system where everyone had access to justice, several academies that dealt with the art and humanities as well as the social sciences and sciences plus he also left behind a large empire making France the dominant European 'power'.

Louis presided over an era of great men, such as Conde, Fouquet, Colbert, Le Tellier and Louvois. It truly was a golden age of politicians- Louis included. Contrary to the view that Louis was an absolutist and a centraliser, he was actually a collaborator who trusted his ministers and the nobles who worked with him to govern and set policies in their respective briefs to make the right calls and right decisions. Louis gave his ministers and nobles that freedom in decision making.

As Wilkinson notes, Louis was a success. He had a 'Bourbon on the throne of Spain', made several territorial gains consolidating French boundaries and presided over an era when French became the 'language of culture and diplomacy'. Wilkinson continues 'Perhaps [Louis'] greatest strengths were his political know-how, his devotion to his dynasty and his flair for publicity'. Louis ran an efficient administration (cf. Wilkinson, Louis xiv), and dedicated himself to making France a great and global power. According to Hassall, Louis can be considered to be a hero, very much like and on a par with the heroic Napoleon Bonaparte (cf. Hassall, Louis xiv). Louis and his royal administration cleaned up France setting her up on a path to glory. As Hassall notes 'the rival power had found France divided, [Louis' administration] gave her a union. [Louis] found France a mere duchy; [he] made her a kingdom. From being composed of nobles and serfs, France became consolidated into a great nation'. Finally, Louis made France the most dominant power in Europe rivalling the likes of the Spanish House of Hapsburgs (cf. Hassall, Louis xiv).

As for the view that the absolutist model that Louis left behind caused the French revolution (cf. Wilkinson, Louis xiv), such a view is unsubstantiated. On the contrary- it was precisely because Louis' successors Louis xvi and Marie Antoinette did not follow Louis' model of consultation and negotiant where he appointed successful ministers who had the freedom to devise and implement policies that caused the revolution to gather pace, that ultimately destroyed the monarchy and France in the process. As Hassall notes, the fault lies with louis' successors, such as Louis xv and Louis xvi due to their failure to be energetic and enlightened administrators (cf. Hassall, Louis xiv). These two kings adopted a laissez faire approach to government rather than copying the interventionist Louis who took all into account and concerned himself with all of the issues France faced. It was the negligence of Louis xv and Louis xvi as well as Marie Antoinette and their lack of interest in the wellbeing of the people that caused the revolution. That negligence can be epitomised by Marie Antoinette's comment: 'Let them eat cake'. Had all these monarchs adopted and followed Louis' model of governance, then it is fair to say that the revolution would not have occurred (cf. Hassall, Louis xiv).

Suffice to say Louis was a talented leader who led his country for the best part of seventy years. He modernised and improved France, the country of his birth which he led with skill and aplomb. For that Louis xiv, king of France should be remembered and warmly congratulated.

BIBLIOGRAPHY

Primary Sources
Primary Sources
Mallia-Milanes, Louis xiv and France
Church, The Greatness of Louis xiv

Secondary Sources
Cronin, Louis xiv
Wilkinson, Louis xiv
Treasure, Louis xiv
Dunlop, Louis xiv
Mitford, The Sun King
Wolf, Louis xiv
Hassall, Louis xiv
Campbell, Louis xiv
Ashley, Louis xiv and the Greatness of France
Mansel, King of the World: The Life of Louis xiv
Wilkinson, Louis xiv: The Real King of Versailles
Harper and Goethe, Louis xiv, the Real Sun King

RICHELIEU

Preface 103

Chapter 1   Origins 107
Chapter 2   Richelieu as First Minister 123
Chapter 3   Richelieu and the nobility.................... 151
Chapter 4   Richelieu and the Huguenots............... 161
Chapter 5   Foreign Policy 167
Chapter 6   Domestics... 173
Chapter 7   Richelieu as Patron 187

Concluding thoughts..207
Bibliography.. 211

PREFACE

I first encountered Armand Jean du Plessis de Richelieu-better known as Cardinal Richelieu as a young child during a tv serialisation of the books of the French writer, Alexander Dumas' 'The Three Musketeers' as well as being a reader of the books by Dumas at school (cf. Dumas, The Three Musketeers, The Man in the Iron Mask, Twenty Years After). Since then I was never to meet Richelieu until I recently wrote a biography of France's king, Louis xiv where I was confronted once again with the figure of Richelieu. This work is an attempt to visit Richelieu and is an attempt to understand one of the most important figures in the history of France.

Richelieu, by Dumas was characterised as a villain. Meanwhile, historians have tended to be far kinder to Richelieu than the fictional tales of Dumas.

This work sets out to contribute to studies about Richelieu and seeks to get at the essence and substance of his character.

I will seek to argue that Richelieu was a highly successful first minister, loyal to the king and his attempts to realise his 'gloire'. He was an incredibly talented and efficient minister and administrator ushering in a new age of greatness for France. Richelieu did much to cultivate the intellectual and cultural life of France- which she still retains till very day in times of modernity.

As we shall see, Richelieu made significant contributions to the Catholic church's counterreformation which was her reply to the Protestant reformation and doctrines of the reformer Martin Luther.

Having descended from a humble background, du Plessis rose to the highest offices of state where he became a cardinal of the roman catholic church, a prince of the church and was first minister of France, the second most important minister and person in the whole of France after the king. Armand conquered two important institutions- the church and the state. He accumulated vast amounts of land and territory in France- it was hard not to escape his presence- such was his dominance and influence in France.

Richelieu through the system of the intendants turned France into a modern bureaucratic nation state. His successors Louis xiv and Cardinal Mazarin capitalised on Richelieu's policies and success- often using the same methods as Richelieu to build up France into said modern nation state.

As we shall see, many of the ideas of Richelieu had long lasting success and long lasting consequences for modern France.

Richelieu was a pivotal figure in the life of France. He was one of the most powerful agents in the world of France- if not the whole of her history. He did much to modernise her institutions which he sharpened up and made more efficient. A lot of the present institutions such as the 'Academie Francaise' owe their presence to the policies of Richelieu- such was his importance, that he could be called the father of the nation.

CHAPTER 1

Origins

Armand-Jean du Plessis de Richelieu (cf. Levi, Cardinal Richelieu and the Making of France), who was to later become Cardinal Richelieu of France was born on 9 September 1585, 'almost certainly in Paris'. Armand was special- he was the fourth and youngest son in a set of five (cf. Bergin, Sturdy, Richelieu and Mazarin, Bergin, Cardinal Richelieu Power and Pursuit of Wealth) of Francois du Plessis, a nobleman from Poitou and Suzanne la Porte (cf. Ferderen, Richelieu), the daughter of Francois de la Porte, a celebrated jurist, barrister in the Parlement of Paris, and the president of the advocates' guild in Poitiers (cf. Knecht, Richelieu, Federen, Richelieu).

Francois was a 'prevot de l'hotel' in which he was responsible for keeping law and order at court. As the historian, Joseph Bergin notes, Francois did much to advance and enhance the position of the du Plessis family- he introduced his family to intrigues both in court politics and the world of finance (cf. Bergin, The Rise of Richelieu)- in that sense Francois was a social climber. In 1578 he assumed the title of 'grand prevot de France' and was created a knight of the Holy Ghost, a new order set up in memory of Henry iii. As a result of his duties, Francois was largely based in Paris, a reason no doubt why his son, Richelieu was born in the location of Paris, capital of France, rather than the family home of Poitou. As part of Henry's team he was involved in all of the major events of the wars of religion, but did not live to see the French victory- Francois passed away on 10 July 1590 at the age of 42. Armand owed much to his father who sparked off his interest in politics of which he would rise to the very top of the political profession.

Suzanne, Richelieu's mother married Francois de Plessis in 1549, bringing him a substantial dowry. Together, they had six children- three sons, Henry, Alphonse-Louis and Armand-Jean, and three daughters, Francoise, Nicole and Isabelle (cf. Sturdy, Richelieu and Mazarin). Armand's earlier brother was to be a courtier, his second brother was destined for the Church. For Armand, his role was to embark on military career (cf. Wedgwood, Richelieu and the French Monarchy).

Suzzanne, then moved with her children back to

Louis XIV and Richelieu

the family and ancestral home based in the chateau (cf. Wedgewood, Richelieu and the French Monarchy) at Poitou, where Armand, her youngest son spent most of his childhood. Armand's uncle, Amador de la Porte, took Armand to Paris at the age of nine (cf. Bergin) where he enrolled at the famous and prestigious College de Navarre- the Eton of its day (cf. Sturdy, Richelieu and Mazarin, Wedgwood, Richelieu and the French Monarchy) where he studied philosophy (cf. Bergin). La Porte, his mother's brother-in-law paid for Armand's education.

After his studies, his mother convened a family council which decided that the next step in Armand's life should be to take up the profession of a soldier- he soon embarked on a military career (cf. Wedgwood). He was entitled with the title 'marquis du Chillou' and was allowed to carry a sword. Armand was ambitious- after moving away from his uncle's home to the home of a parliamentier called Bouthillier, he joined the Academy of Antoine de Pluvinel, a finishing school for young noblemen. As well as physical exercises, fencing and riding, the school educated Richelieu in social manners and social etiquette. The school informed the young Armand on how to dress appropriately at court. The school was to have a long lasting effect on du Plessis' career where he used what he had learnt at the school to inform his behaviour at court with the king.

As a result of the family's fortuitous luck in acquiring the bishopric of Lucon which Henry III granted the family (cf. Sturdy, Richelieu and Mazarin, Bergin). Lucon granted the family a steady stream of income. Richelieu's mother wanted his brother Alphonse to train for the position of bishop, but Alphonse had no ambitions or intentions to embark on such a highly pressured role and instead became a Carthusian monk (cf. Bergin). It then fell to Armand to take up a leading clerical position in the church. It was decided that Armand should undertake religious instructions and training, diverting him away from his career in the army. The decision to take up Holy Orders was very much the idea of Armand who in a stunning volte face told his family that he wished to embark on a career as a religious figure (cf. Wedgwood, Richelieu and the French Monarchy). The change in career, necessitated a change in education. At the age of nine, accompanied by his uncle Armand de la Porte left Pluvinels Academy, the base of his military training and took up his studies at the prestigious College de Navarre- the Eton of its day to study philosophy. Armand took up his new studies with relish and eagerness. The course was composed of three main subjects: grammar, arts and philosophy. Armand was ambitious and bright. He took his studies seriously- he was meticulous to a fault- he did not take criticism well but when he was informed as to his mistakes- he would be quick to rectify and correct himself. As an early biographer notes: 'his thirst for praise and fear of criticism were such as to keep him fully stretched' (cf. Knecht, Richelieu). The intenseness and difficulty of his studies has been attributed as the cause of the enduring cause of Armand's poor health. Armand was soon appointed bishop of Lucon by Henry iv in 1606 (cf. Bergin), hence inheriting his family's seat and base of power and influence. Because of his young age, upon which he was below the canonical age of bishop, the Pope granted Armand a dispensation, allowing him to become bishop at the young age of twenty-one (cf. Sturdy, Richelieu and Mazarin). At just twenty-one years of age, du Plessis 'was among France's youngest, best educated, and almost certainly, [one of its] ambitious bishops' (cf. Bergin, Cardinal Richelieu: power and pursuit of wealth)- in other word- du Plessis was the leader of his generation. Armand left France, for Rome. He reached the Holy City in January 1607 and was introduced to Pope Paul V by the French ambassador. Armand acquired proficiency in Italian and Spanish. Now that Armand had received his dispensation from Pope Paul V, he was consecrated as bishop in Rome on 17 April 1907. Armand had arrived- he never looked back.

Armand returned to Paris in order to fulfil the completion of his studies. On 29 October, he was awarded the BA in Theology. As a theology student, he received tuition from Gabriel de L'Aubespine, a member of the clergy, six years his senior. 'L'Aubespine came from a family of royal officers and magistrates who had long standing relations with Armand's family (cf. Marvick, The Young Monarch). He was admitted to the prestigious Sorbonne. Although he was now ready to assume his role at court, an illness befell Armand. For several weeks he suffered from bouts of fever and severe headaches. By Lent, his health had significantly improved enough for Armand at the invitation of the king to preach at court. However, feeling underappreciated, Armand returned to his diocese. The Plessis family, benefited significantly from Lucon- they received income from Lucon however, its cathedral and episcopal palace had fallen into a mess and a state. Richelieu, as we shall soon learn, was to set himself the task of improving both the cathedral and the Palais-Cardinale.

Richelieu set himself the task of forming a base befitting and worthy of his role as bishop. He employed servants, acquired furniture and within a few months, he became a figure of note and substance. He was installed as bishop and promised to serve his flock with compassion and diligence.

Richelieu took up his new role with relish involving and engaging himself in the counter-reformation that was taking place within the catholic church and was the church's response to the Protestantism of Martin Luther. He was the first and most prominent bishop to support the reforms to the church suggested at the Council of Trent and duly implemented the reforms that Trent had suggested (cf. Bergin). Richelieu was loyal to the church and did all in his powers to improve the church in her new lease and springs of intellectual and cultural life. As Sturdy notes not only did the reformers tackle and deal with the problem of heresy, the movement revived spirituality and social action among the clergy and the laity (cf. Sturdy, Richelieu and Mazarin). As part of Armand's contribution to the counter reformation, a synod was established at Lucon. The council issued a set of policies that would improve the state of the catholic church in France. In order to improve the quality of the clergy, priests were to stay away from amenities such as fairs and abstain from trade and games of chance. All were expected to dress decently worthy of their role as god's servants. Priests were required to take the administration of sacraments seriously and observe the liturgy of the mass in a diligent manner. Pubs were to be closed during services. All parish priests were required to teach the catechism and were required to cite the Lord's Prayer and the Ten Commandments in the vernacular rather than French. Restrictions were loosened regarding the laity's reception of communion- they were required to take communion at least once and month, and at least on one of the four major feast days of the Christian year. Richelieu is an important figure in the life of the Catholic church where many of his policies contributed to the revival of the church.

Richelieu embarked on improving the spiritual life of inhabitants of his diocese. As part of his contribution to the counter reformation he wrote and composed a small catechism, called the 'Instruction du Chretien' which aimed to present catholic doctrine, in an accessible manner for the church's members and followers. Though not inclined to the austerity of ascetic life embraced by the likes of Ignatious of Loyola, Therese of Avila and John of the Cross who are usually associated with the counterreformation, Armand was dedicated to the improvement of the church- 'he devoutly believed in the Roman Church's great mission and repeatedly sought to improve it institutional functioning and to abet its religious purposes'. The 'Instruction' was a success, achieving a wide readership in France and was translated into several languages.

Richelieu as part of the counter reformation movement opened a seminary for the training of the clergy, strove to improve the intellectual and spiritual quality of the clergy, embarked on several visits to the parishes of the diocese, 'and encouraged the attendance at Mass by the laity'. For inspiration Richelieu turned to two figures who would later play a crucial role in his later career- they were Pierre de Berulle and Francois le Clerc du Tremblay, known as Pere Joseph. Having taken a dislike to the 'traditional monastic vows, and the exception of the monasteries from episcopal jurisdiction', du Plessis sought to invite the Oratorians, an order known for being secular in the sense that they were not bound by monastic vows to establish themselves in France. Berulle was responsible for the introduction of the Oratorians to said France- a catholic order inspired by the thoughts of St Phillip Neri (cf. Levi, Cardinal Richelieu and the Making of France) in 1611. Richelieu first introduced to Oratorians to Paris before establishing them in his own diocese of Lucon. Armand also sought to introduce congregations which were not exempt from his jurisdiction, including the likes of the order of the Visitations soon to be founded by Jeanne-Francioise de Chantal and Francois de Sales, 'for specific pastoral purposes (cf. Levi, Cardinal Richelieu and the Making of France). Berulle was eventually made a cardinal. The second figure was Pere Joseph who was a Capuchin monk, who before becoming a priest, worked in the army and embarked on diplomatic business for the crown. As well as being a reformer, he also sought to convert the protestant Huguenots to Catholicism, through missionaries. Richelieu in his later dealings with the Huguenots was to model his dealings with them based on Pere Joseph's strategy (cf. Sturdy, Richelieu and Mazarin).

Meanwhile, Henry iv passed away in 1610- his widow, Marie de Medici, was left to rule France as regent (cf. Treasure, Cardinal Richelieu and the Development of Absolutism) assisting their son, the new king, Louis xiii. The Bourbons were becoming powerful- there was a 'double marriage', between Louis xiii and Anne, the Spanish Infanta, and Louis' sister, Elizabeth and Philip, heir to the Spanish throne (cf. Treasure, Cardinal Richelieu and the development of Absolutism, Wedgewood, Richelieu and the French Monarchy). The king's cousin and heir presumptive, Conde opposed the marriage and openly threatened to take over the throne. Marie sought to convene an Estates General in a bid to deal with and resolve the conde problem. It was to prove to be the last meeting before the revolution. Henry during his reign, had never convened a council. Before 1560, when it was called after the sudden death of Henry II, the council had not met for the best part of sixty-six years; in the reigns of his sons, Francis II, Charles ix and Henry III, it became the vehicle for catholic and Huguenot grievances (cf. Treasure, Cardinal Richelieu and the development of Absolutism).

Richelieu was talent spotted by the dauphin's mother

Louis XIV and Richelieu

and regent, Queen Marie de Medici and the clergy of Poitou who invited Armand to speak at the Estates General on their behalf- he was young- just twenty-nine years old (cf. Bergin, Levi, Cardinal Richelieu and the Making of France). The Estates were composed of three estates – the church, the nobility and the third estate- that is to say the rest- or commoners if you will (cf. Sturdy, Richelieu and Mazarin). At the meeting, Armand noted that in order to improve the crown's financial situation, useless gifts should be restricted, there should be less tax exemptions and the quality of the clergy should be improved. The church, according to Armand 'was deprived of all honour, robbed of its wealth, denied authority and profaned'- and thus should be exempt from paying taxes. Armand also suggested that bishops should have more political and state power. Armand provided four solutions which would improve the state of the church. First the clergy should be given a role in the governance of the country. There was precedent for the practice- Christian clergy in the past had always helped the state. Secondly, the church should be exempt from paying taxes. Third it should be buffered from attacks by lay judges and others. The Huguenots who resorted to violence should be duly punished, whilst the peaceful ones should be left in peace. Last, the king should be informed and guided by the gospels.

Members of the estates were impressed by Richelieu's

conduct and speeches to the extent that he was invited to give the closing speech of the council (cf. Sturdy, Richelieu and Mazarin).

Historians such as Joseph Bergin have noted that there wasn't anything significant about Richelieu's role at the Estates General, were it not for the fact that he was chosen by the clergy to speak on their behalf, he might not have attracted such attention (cf. Bergin, The Rise of Richelieu). That is not strictly true- Richelieu's assured performance at the Estates attracted and impressed the Queen Mother who kept him on the radar and would later invite Richelieu to take up some government tasks.

After the Estates, the Queen Regent began to make extensive use of Richelieu involving him in the intrigues and diplomacy of court and sent Armand on several errands of state. He was appointed to serve the Queen-Mother's favourite, Concino Concini, the most powerful minister in the whole of France at that time (cf. Pardoe). He was also sent to pacify and neutralise the king's rebellious cousin, the Prince de Conde. A few months later, he was made ambassador to Spain. This last role did not come to fruition since Armand was appointed to the Council of State, as secretary of state, responsible for foreign affairs (cf. Wedgwood, Richelieu and the French Monarchy). He soon became, like Concini, one of the Queen Mother's closest advisors.

Louis XIV and Richelieu

After an internal dispute, when Mangot was appointed to fill the seat of Keeper of the Seals, this left the post of secretary of state vacant. Richelieu was then appointed as Secretary of State on 30 November 1616, with special responsibility for foreign affairs (cf. Treasure, Cardinal Richelieu and the Development of Absolutism). Richelieu was amongst powerful people- he never let go of them.

One of Armand's first tasks was to deal with aristocratic rebellions. Armand responded by quickly convening three armies under the duc de Guise, the comte d'Auvegne and marshal Montigny, respectively. More investigation needs to be taken as to how the rebellion was dealt with. In foreign affairs Armand sought to reassure France's former protestant allies- England, the United Provinces and the German princes that, Marie de Medic's recent dalliances with Hapsburgs did not mean that France had forgotten her former allies. Armand dispatched several agents to pronounce on the queen's policies.

Armand soon fell out of favour- in a reshuffle he was dismissed from his ministerial post, after a dispute at court concerning the king, his mother and her favourite Concini (cf. Pardoe). Many of the positions were occupied by Henry iv's previous ministers, Villeroy, Jeannin, du Vair and Sillery. He also ceased to be a royal councillor. At the dispatch of Concini, Richelieu too lost power, having lost a valuable ally in Concini (cf. Parker). After the dispute with his mother, the king banished Marie de Marie to Blois whilst Richelieu accompanied her as president of her council. Richelieu was out in the cold, for the best part of seven years (cf. Sturdy, Richelieu and Mazarin). However, he did not waste his time whilst in exile- he dutifully composed a catechism, entitled 'L'Instruction du chretien (cf. Bergin).

After years of being in the wilderness, Richelieu made a spectacular comeback. In 1619, the Queen Mother managed to escape the Chateau de Blois and became head of a rebellion aimed at the king. The king then appointed Richelieu to deal as mediator between the regent and her son. The negotiations ended in the enactment of the 'Treaty of Angouleme' which back the Queen Mother her full powers and was restored to her position as a member of the royal council. Richelieu then resigned his seat at Lucon, so that he could attend his new duties as a member of the king's council. He reserved for himself an annuity of 5,000 livres out of the Lucon seat. He also ceased to be Marie's Grand Almoner (cf. Knecht, Richelieu). Further luck and good fortune were to come Armand's way. Louis had sought to maintain continuity by appointing and keeping his father's ministers in power however they were thinning out. Villeroy had passed away in 1617. Jeannin was eighty, as was the new Keeper of the Seals, De Vic, Chancellor Sillery's son, Puysieuex, were not that

Louis XIV and Richelieu

competent. The head of the council, the cardinal de Retz was only in position by title alone- no substance as it were. There were only two men of note- the prince of Conde and the finance minister Schomberg. Conde was released from captivity and was admitted to the council. Schomberd was competent but had failed to curtail state expenditure. Meanwhile, Louis nominated Richelieu for the position of cardinal which Pope Gregory xv accordingly granted in September 1622 (Knecht, 9 January 2014). Richelieu was consecrated as cardinal on 5th September 1622. Following his promotion to the position of cardinal Richelieu joined the three former figures where he was admitted to the king's council (cf. Dyer, 1861). On the 12th August of the same year, after the resignation Louis's first minister, Charles Le Vieuville due to charges of corruption, Richelieu took his position of principal minister, though the Cardinal de la Rochefoucauld nominally remained president of the council. However, Richelieu in November, 1629 Richelieu was appointed president of the council. Richelieu had arrived.

CHAPTER 2

Richelieu as First Minister

The relationship between Richelieu and Louis determined not only the trajectory of France but also determined the future of Western Europe and the trajectory that she would take in the present and future whilst remaining loyal to her glorious past. Both Louis and Richelieu arrived at a time when Catholics and Protestants were in opposition to one another. They also arrived at the time when the catholic church was undergoing her internal reformation with the counter reformation which was a response to the protestant reformation of Martin Luther (cf. Wedgwood, Richelieu and the French Monarchy). Richelieu was faced with an intray where he was called upon to deal with France's political, social and economic problems as well as her international and foreign adventures. His two chief aims were to centralise power in France and amount a formidable opposition to the growing powers and influence of the Hapsburg family- both in Austria and Spain (cf. Wedgwood). Now that he was first minister, Richelieu needed a power base and nerve centre from which he could govern France. This he did by constructing the Palais-Cardinal, which became and was appropriated by the king once Richelieu's rule had ended and became known as the Palais-Royal (cf. Alexander). He also built the Chateau-Richelieu as well as the town of Richelieu.

Richelieu was met with a burgeoning in-tray upon his accession to first minister of state. As the historian Robin Briggs notes, amongst the letters of congratulation that greeted Richelieu was one by a future surintendant d'Effiat who diagnosed France's problems to which Richelieu set himself the task of resolving. According to d'Ettiat, there was a decline in royal authority, division in the church, France had a protestant problem, had trouble with the behaviour of the nobles, was confronted with the issue of the sale of offices, merchants who were leaving the profession to secure offices, the state of revenue and expenditure and there was an issue concerning the payment of pensions when the nobility retired (cf. Bergin, Brockliss, Richelieu and his Age). Richelieu's rule as first minister was to deal with and tackle each of these issues, head on- which for the most part he did with efficiency and competence.

The conseil d'en haut, admitted Armand on 29 April 1624, the highest policy making body in France. It formed part of the king's council, also comprised of three lesser councils- the Conseil d'etat, Conseil des finances and Conseil prive'. These councils each had their own responsibilities- including administration, finance and justice – though they overlapped and interacted with one another. The Conseil d'etat were administrative councils, which put into effect the decisions that the king had taken. The main bodies were the conseil de finances, which after restructuring in 1615, assessed and collated taxation and dealt with the financial affairs of state, the counsel prive later known as the conseil des parties, which dealt mainly with administration and the conseil des depeches, which oversaw the transmission of royal laws and the other instructions to provincial bodies and assemblies. Apart from the king, its members were ministers and included the chief minister, the chancellor or Keeper of the Seals, the minister of finance (surinintendant des finances) and at least one secretary of state (cf. Sturdy, Richelieu and Mazarin). Together these councils gave birth to France as a burgeoning bureaucratic nation state.

More often than not, the king sat and presided over the council. When absent, his place was occupied by his mother or the chancellor. All decisions were taken- ex cathedra if you will by 'the king in his council'. Louis had free reign and total control over the decisions of the councils- he was free to veto their decisions if he did not agree with their proposals. His decisions were set out in decrees, had the force of law, no other authority could override their decisions- not even the courts- only the king could veto or amend the enacted legislation (cf. Knecht, Richelieu). Louis ran an efficient and tight ship.

By the time, Richelieu had joined the king's council, La Vieuville, who had been finance minister since January 1623. La Vieuville soon proved an unpopular figure in the whole of France, due to his unpopular financial polices. Richelieu said of him, he was 'like a drunkard who could not take a step without fumbling' (cf. Knecht, Richelieu). La Vieuville fell out of favour with the king- he offered to resign, but the king 'preferred to arrest him'. In an inspired decision by Louis the next day, Richelieu was appointed Chief Minister. Louis' chose to appoint the catholic cardinal in order to substantiate France as the leading catholic country. This was to prove fortuitous since Lous' son and successor, Louis xiv was gifted the title of 'Most Christian King' by the Pope. Richelieu had arrived.

According to the historian, Lloyd Moote, there was no 'formal office or charge of prime ministre'. Richelieu

Louis XIV and Richelieu

according to Moote, had no conciliar title other than minister of state, though his colleagues did address him as 'le premier minister de l'etat' (cf. Bergin and Brockliss, Richelieu and his Age).

Richelieu approached his work as minister with great diligence, informed as he was by his philosophical and theological training as priest and cardinal. The abundance of his correspondence, his 'Memoirs' and his 'Political Testament' speak of a minister who was dedicated to the art of politics. As the historian David J Sturdy notes Richelieu developed into a 'master politician in a 'technical sense", that is to say he was highly efficient and adept at handling any political issue that came his way (cf. Sturdy, Richelieu and Mazarin). As Sturdy notes, Richelieu's arrival on the French and European stage came at a time when the France began to enjoy her own scientific revolution. Philosophers such as Rene Descartes and Pierre Gassendi were prominent in the scientific revolution where for example the former developed the scientific subject and practice of mathematics. Groups of philosophers and scientists frequently met up regularly in Paris from 1620s and 1630s where they discussed the latest ideas in science and epistemology (cf. Sturdy, Richelieu and Mazarin). The conventional view is that during the renaissance there was a rupture and growing dissonance between philosophy and the new subject of science. Far from it- both reason and science, philosophy and the natural sciences, worked in tandem with one another, in mutual sympathy and mutual harmony with one another. Richelieu in his patronage of these new men of philosophy and science spearheaded France as a modern and dynamic nation state where she gained a self confidence and self identity that had previously eluded her.

As Chief Minister Richelieu pretty much had authority over the whole of France. He was the king's deputy- as it were, but the two according to the historians, R J Knecht and Sturdy were not close- they were temperamentally incompatible- Richelieu was never the king's favourite. Despite Richelieu turning on the charm, Louis did not reciprocate. Louis found his chief minister a 'forbidding presence and the possessor of an overpowering personality'. Nevertheless, Louis knew talent when he saw it- he maintained and kept Richelieu in power- there relationship was very much a professional one- which accordingly flourished (cf. Knecht, Richelieu, Sturdy, Richelieu and Mazarin). Richelieu as a result of his position as Chief minister, had creative freedom with respect to the governance of France. As long as he was supported by the king, he could do anything he wanted to within the bounds of reason.

The two- Louis and Richelieu had a successful working political relationship and relationship- though

Louis XIV and Richelieu

personally they were not especially close, though their professional partnership was a successful one. Louis xiii applied himself to the task of governance whilst he took Richelieu's policy proposals seriously and in an informed manner implemented those policies suggested by Richelieu suggested to him accordingly after going a process of evaluation. Though he rarely attended the royal court unless for reasons of government duties, his poor health confined him to bed though he maintained correspondence via letters. As early as the summer of 1625 he notified the king:

'I have not the words to acknowledge the honour that your majesty does me in all respects, and even when the day comes that I have as much good health as I now have bad, my actions will not be sufficient to do so. What consoles me, Sire, is that…healthy or unwell…I will have no thought, movement or action which does not have your service at aim' (cf. Sturdy, Richelieu and Mazarin).

Louis was considerate of his first minister's health, 'absolving him from having meetings with visitors, petitioners or other individuals who took up the cardinal's time'. A letter from the king to Richelieu, notes that he sought to relieve Richelieu of some of his minor duties, so that he could concentrate on the more important affairs of state. Nevertheless at times when the king required Richelieu's presence even if he was not well, the king's demands of his minister's presence overrode his own minister's health- such was the importance of Richelieu to Louis's plans for his kingdom. For example Louis required Richelieu to accompany him on military campaigns. At the siege of La Rochelle in 1628, Richelieu was with him despite the bad weather which took a toll on the latter's health (cf. Sturdy, Richelieu and Mazarin). The cardinal recovered.

As Wedgwood, notes Richelieu's policy involved two goals- the centralisation of power in France, and to check opposition to the Hapsburg dynasty, which ruled in both Spain and Austria.

Richelieu had plans for France. In that sense he was ambitious for France. He sought to protect and balance the crown's royal prerogative against the demands and interest of the aristocracy, parlements, provincial agents and other 'intermediate' legal bodies. He constantly applied himself to matters such as how the king could achieve prestige both domestically and abroad; how to finance the exploits of government, how to respond to rebellions and protest which threatened social cohesion, he applied himself to how to deal with the Huguenots, whose presence challenged the stability of the Catholic church and its ability to unify the country, as well as how to preserve the king's 'gloire' as King of France,

Louis XIV and Richelieu

especially against the Huguenots (cf. Sturdy, Richelieu and Mazarin).

As part of his plans to centralise power in France, Richelieu engaged in selling offices, something that his successors Mazarin and Louis xiv continued to practice in order to fund and increase the crown's coffers. The majority of personal who populated the law courts or the fiscal institutions of the state, and held other public positions were officiers who had bought their posts. This practice went as far back as the fifteenth century but intensified under the rule of Richelieu. The sale of officers was a useful and efficient method of raising finances to fund the king's policies and activities and fill said royal coffers. So widespread was the practice, that a whole department- the recette des parties casuelles in 1522 was set up to specifically deal with the sale of offices. Whereas in 1515, there were some 4000-5000 officiers in France, the number had risen to 25,000 by 1610 and had further increased under Louis xiii and Luis xiv. By the early 1660s there were some 46,000 officiers, a sufferable amount, that Louis xiv's minister Jean-Baptiste Colbert sought to restrict the number of officiers. The sale of offices was a spectacular success- not only was it an effective and efficient method of raising finances, it also conferred on its purchasers 'social status and opened up routes both to social ascension and to careers that wee handsomely rewarded (cf. Sturdy, Richelieu and Mazarin).

To further consolidate power in France, Richelieu sought to curb the powers of the feudal nobility. In 1626, he abolished the Constable of France and ordered all fortified castles to be struck down, except those needed to defend against invaders (cf. Collins). He stripped the princes, dukes, and lesser aristocrats of defences which could have been deployed in rebellion against the king- the nobility were emasculated.

France under the rule of Richelieu became a modern and bureaucratic nation state. As well as the councils, both Richelieu and his successor Cardinal Jules Mazarin used the system of intendants to wield their powers over France. The intendants were special commissioners who were the 'eyes and ears of government' (cf. Campbell-Bannerman, Louis xiv), sent out to ensure that royal decrees were duly enforced in all of the localities of France. Their prime purpose according to Knecht was to remove all opposition to the war effort. Knecht continues: had it not been for the prolific use of the intendants during the war years, it is difficult to see how France could have emerged from the Thirty Wars Year with success- though Richelieu himself did not live long enough to see said war to completion (cf. Knecht, Richelieu). As the historians Knecht and Sturdy note, the intendants were not a new creation as such- they had been around as far back as the thirteenth and fourteenth centuries where they were sent out to provinces to enforce the royal will. According to Sturdy the intendants were around as long as the middle ages, though their roles developed and changed over time. From the 1550s, the crown appointed advisers (intendants) to assist and help provincial governors with financial administration- they were usually drawn from the legal profession or civil servants from the government central council. Secondly, during the wars of religion, the crown sent commissioners again from the law courts or royal council on missions to scrutinise and supervise the various edicts that were being handed out. Thirdly, Henri continued with the policy of dispatching intendants to oversee the implementation of the Edict of Nantes and to assist financiers in their duties. By the time Louis xiii and Louis xiv came to the throne the role of the intendants was mainly 'advisory or supervisory' (cf. Sturdy, Richelieu and Mazarin). Richelieu and Louis through their extensive use of intendants professionalised them and made them more effective and efficient in terms of collecting taxes and revenue for the crown's coffers. It was the increasing and intensified use of the intendants that first occurred under Louis xiii and Louis xiv that marks out the latter intendants from their early days colleagues- if you will. Under Louis xiii and Richelieu's rule, according to Sturdy, the intendants were drawn from the legal profession where they often completed the task allocated to them by the king and first minister before returning to their every day job and work. According to Knecht the intendants came into their own under the ruler of Richelieu. They were luckier than the officiers- they had sufficient powers, albeit with the proviso that said powers could be revoked at any time if they failed in their duties (cf. Knecht, Richelieu). It was not until the time of Louis xiv and his first minister, Mazarin, that the intendants became a separate class and institution in its own right becoming a profession all of its own (cf. Knecht, Richelieu, Sturdy, Richelieu and Mazarin).

As first minister, Richelieu gave detailed instructions to ambassadors, military commanders and provisional governors. He maintained a huge correspondence with bishops, nobles, office holders and intendants. In June 1626 he was discharged from hearing grievances in order to allow him to concentrate on more important affairs of state. He was very much the dominant voice in council. He did not attend the minor councils but was kept abreast of their operations informed by the chancellor. Given that he was not competent in terms of financial policy- he delegated such matters to others. For a long time historians have believed that Richelieu governed France on his own. That is strictly not true. He often

Louis XIV and Richelieu

appointed men who were to assist him in the governance of France. His assistants were known as his 'creatures'. As he himself gathered offices and wealth, the Plessis and the La Portes gained positions of powers and influence. Richeliue's brother, like Richelieu was appointed as cardinal, one niece a duchess and a cousin, a marshal of France. Countless members of Richelieu's family were granted positions of power, hence legitimating and strengthening Richelieu's sphere of power. One significant family that benefited from Richelieu's patronage were the Bouthilliers. In September 1628 Claude Bouthillier became secretary of state, and in May 1629 he succeeded to the department of foreign affairs. In 1632, leon, his son, comte de Chavigny, became secretary of state for foreign affairs, while his father and Claude de Builon became finance ministers. The Bouthelliers family remained the favourite set of familial collaborators of Richelieu's right till the end of his professional career. After 1630 according to Knecht, Richelieu switched from dealing with domestic affairs to dealing with foreign affairs- he left the operation of domestic affairs in the hands of others. That is not quite true- though Richelieu delegated matters to other ministers, he kept abreast of and was fully informed of their policies and plans. As Bergin notes, 'routine matters of administration' 'he left to those employed for that purpose, but the decisions which shaped the history of his wealth were his alone' (cf. Knecht, Richelieu).

As Knecht, notes Richelieu used his assistants, the four secretaries of state to assist him in the governance of France. Previously their role was to make sure that the king's requests received concrete form and shape- for example, they read to the king, his correspondence and created letters at the king's dictation. By the time of seventeenth century- that is to say, in Richelieu's time, the secretariat had further developed where the secretaries toured the country and reported to the king and the chief minister the occurrences in France. The secretaries, as Knecht, notes were also intermediaries between the king and the chief minister keeping their lines of communication open. Louis always had a secretary at the ready who would inform the king's colleagues as to his trajectory of policy. Chavigny, a secretary of state's reports were gratefully received by Richelieu since it kept him abreast of affairs of state as well as the current mood and feelings of the king- 'if the king continues to keep his disposition on the plate where it is now', he wrote on 3 September 1638, 'His Eminence should have no difficulty in proposing whatever he pleases to him, for his Majesty will not make any opposition to following his advice, and I see that at this moment he is out of that distrustful mood which he expressed in the past'.

Louis XIV and Richelieu

As secretary of state for foreign affairs, Chavigny had two main duties- to keep the lines of communication through correspondence between governments and their ambassadors. Second he had the duty of contributing to the development of foreign policy decisions. Perhaps one of the most competent secretary of state was Francois Sublet de Noyers who was responsible for war and took up the position in 1636. If not quite well regarded by Louis, for Richelieu he was one of his most trusted informers. He was a diligent worker where for the best part of seven years he prepared some 18,000 letters and dispatches. Unlike other secretaries, Francois' interests and responsibilities were wide ranging- he attended to a large number of business, and military affairs. He was the middle man between army officers who sought to have increased pay, and the finance ministers, 'who tried to avoid paying for' said pay and salary. Richelieu noted of him 'I have so much faith in what comes from Monsieur de Noyers' 'that is not necessary for him to send me musters and troop reviews which he well knows that I never see. It is sufficient that he take the trouble to write me what is happening'. Sublet was duly promoted and rewarded by Richelieu- he became superindentent of royal buildings, and as such, kept watch on the Louvre. 'He was also concierge of Fontainebleau and in 1642 founded a library for Richelieu and was involved in preparing the cardinal's last will and testament' (cf. Knecht, Richelieu).

Richelieu was very much a conservative, in the traditionalist sense. As Sturdy notes, in social thought, he believed that social hierarchy, just as monarchic government, was divinely ordained- in short he was a fervent supporter of the principle of the divine right of kings. Ideally, there should be a hierarchical account of society. The basic social division was that between clergy, nobility and third estate. He didn't stop there. There was also a hierarchy inter-alia these groups. The clergy had its own hierarchy of archbishops, bishops and so on; the nobility had its hierarchy of titles, whilst the third estate had its own hierarchical structures. Accordingly, the monarch and the first minister should preserve or restore traditional social structures. The Catholic Church had a role to play too- she must urge peace and tranquillity amongst all in society whilst respecting the hierarchies in society, esteeming the rich and comforting those below (cf. Sturdy, Richelieu and Mazarin).

As Richelieu became more confident as chief minister, he sought to rule and call his style of governance, 'raison d'etat'- that is to say 'Reason of State'. This was controversial because the idea and concept was usually and typically associated with the political theory of renaissance thinker Nicolo Machiavelli. According to

Louis XIV and Richelieu

Machiavelli, the sovereign ruler should do all in his powers to maintain his authority over his principality- even if it meant, his policies was deemed immoral or criminal by the populace. The ruler- the prince was not bound by any authority, whether that be ''constitutional', religious, legal or moral". Richelieu was careful to distance himself from Machiavelli's interpretation of the concept, where Richelieu sought to reassure the French populace that his 'raison' policy was quite different from that envisaged by Machiavelli. For Richelieu the practice of the 'raison' was very much 'compatible with Catholic doctrine and conventional ethical norms' (cf. Sturdy, Richelieu and Mazarin). For Richelieu, 'rasion d'etat' simply meant that France should be pragmatic and not ideological when dealing with her domestic and international affairs.

Before Louis had his son, Louis xiv, his brother, Gaston Duc d'Orleans, who before the birth of the dauphin, was the next line in throne and heir presumptive. Once he reached his eighteenth birthday in 1626, Louis xiii and Richelieu sought to marry him to an heiress of the wealthy Montpensier family. If he had children, then the Bourbon dynasty would be preserved and kept in tact. The arrangement was opposed by the conde family, who were the king's cousins, who had a hidden agenda and motive for preventing the marriage. If both Lous and Gaston were childless, the chance of a conde succession would be strengthened. The Conde family was supported by the likes of the Duchess de Chevreuse and Gaston's governor, Jean-Baptiste d'Ornano, Comte de Montlaur. Richelieu persuaded Louis to dispose of the opposition by having Ornano and several of his followers and supporters arrested. He then brought to of his own supporters into the council: Michel de Marillac and Antoine Coiffier de Ruze, Marquis d'Effiat, the latter of whom was the father of Cinq-Mars. Gaston's marriage went ahead where he married Marie de Montpensier on 6 August 1626, and later in the year, there was a clear out- a night of the long knives if you will. There were several arrests, which included the Vendome brothers (the natural sons of Henry iv), the Comte de Soissons, and Henri de Talleyrand, Comte de Chalais (who was implicated in a plot to assassinate Richelieu and was executed) (cf. Sturdy, Richelieu and Mazarin).

For the best part of six years, from April 1624 until November 1630 France was ruled by the triumvirate of the king, his mother and Richelieu. But in November Louis was forced against his own will to drop one of the three, after a territorial dispute concerning the battle between France and the Hapsburg family, over the family's growing influence in northern Italy. The 'Day of the Dupes' is known as the day when Louis made his final decision. For Richelieu the day was to prove and mark

Louis XIV and Richelieu

a decisive and turning point in his career (cf. Knecht, Richelieu). There was an internal dispute involving Louis xiii, his mother, Queen Marie over the status of Richelieu's role as first minister. His position was being threatened by the regent and others such as Marillac. Richelieu at the advice of his friend, Cardinal de Valette, convened a meeting with the king. After a four hour talk, Louis made a decision. He decided to keep hold of Richelieu in what was a stunning act of loyalty and endorsement from the king to his most important minister. Richelieu was back (cf. Sturdy, Richelieu and Mazarin).

In order to guarantee and consolidate his position as first minister, Richelieu was ruthless and capitalised on the 'day of dupes' by purging the country of all opposition, getting rid of all those who had threatened his position. Marillac was imprisoned, his brother Louis, a commander of French forces based in Italy was tried and dispatched. Gaston went on a self-imposed exile and went to Lorraine. The Queen Mother was detained in Compiegne, though she fled to settle in Brussels. Her household was ransacked by Richelieu, which he duly filled with his own supporters. Francois de Bassompiere, confident of the queen mother and Gaston were imprisoned in the Bastille where they remained for twelve years. The Duc d'Elbeuf lost his governorship of Picardy, whilst other members of the nobility were dealt with- often in a hard manner (cf. Sturdy, Richelieu and Mazarin). Henri, duc de Montmorency who caused an uprising in 1632, was executed by Richelieu in 1634; the cardinal's outspoken critic, Urbain Grandier was burnt at the stake. Richelieu further tightened his grip on France by operating a network of spies in the land, so that he could have a knowledge and keep abreast of affairs in France.

Richelieu's powers were growing. Now that he was first minister, he did all in his powers to increase and maintain his grip on France. In this sense he was supported by Louis and the Queen Mother, who were not afraid and perfectly relaxed with du Plessis getting filthy rich. He sought to acquire and improve land, areas and provinces of his governorship. He mainly concentrated on provinces and towns in western France. He started off with Le Havre (October 1626) and spent the rest of his life transforming it into France's strongest fortified town. Other towns followed, such as Harfleur, Monvillers, Pont-de-l'Arche and Honfleur. In late 1626, he gained control of Brouage and transferred control and supervision to the king's mother, Marie de Medici. He became governor in December 1630 of Rez, Aunis and La Rochelle in place of Toiras who was duly compensated with a marshal's baton. In 1632, Richelieu obtained Nantes. He also accepted the governorship of Brittnay at the request of its provincial estates. The most important governorship was Britany, since it carried powers- both discretionary and otherwise and prerogatives dating back to the days of the powerful dukes. In less than six years Richelieu had substantively increased his powers and presence in France. France was becoming the cardinal's personal fiefdom. He also sought to influence his family's sphere of influence by granting members of his family and his political associates, territories and governorships such as Brest and Calais, which extensively increased his power in France. As one historian notes, Richelieu's 'determination and ability to build a power base for himself beyond the court and the council chamber' (cf. Knecht, Richelieu). A significantly large part of France was under the political control of Richelieu. He didn't stop there. According to Knecht, Richelieu was a great purchaser of land. He concentrated on western France where he acquired Anjou-Poitou and Aunis-Saintongne. As one historian puts it: his purchases were 'part of a concentrated strategy aimed at capturing all the important sources of power control in those regions'. Richelieu spent his time accumulating vast amounts of territory and chateaus across France. In 1623 he bought the chateau of Limours, but after only three and a half years, he sold it back to the king. In 1628 the queen mother gifted him the chateau of Bois-le-Vicomte as a present for his success in the capture of La Rochelle where he 'carried out improvements to the building and the park'. Soon Blois became surplus to requirements since it was inconveniently located so Richelieu then rented the chateau of Fleury-en-Biere, where he often stayed for the best part of ten years. Richelieu did not stop there- in 1633 he bought the chateau of Rueil, near Paris. With help from the builder, Jean Thiriot, Richelieu carried out improvements to both chateau and park. He also enlarged the court so that it could accommodate many of his followers (cf. Knecht, Richelieu). As John Evelyn, a visitor to Rueil noted in 1644:

'The house is small, but fairly built in form of a castle, moated around. The offices were towards the road, and over against it are large vineyards, walled in. But though the house is not of the greatest, the gardens about it are so magnificent that I doubt whether Italy has any exceeding I for all rarities of pleasure'.

According to the historian Joseph Bergin, the purchasing of land was not 'the sole object of Richelieu's attention'. Through his professional career he involved himself in other investments such as 'governorships, royal domain, rentes, residences etc- as well as spending great amounts on different building projects' (cf. Bergin, Cardinal Richelieu, Power and Pursuit of Wealth). That is not strictly true- the vast amounts of territory that Richelieu purchased is evidence that Richelieu took his ownership of land seriously, which he used to increase his general powers and influence over France.

Richelieu's growing power did not concern Louis so

Louis XIV and Richelieu

much- he was perfectly secure in his own position as king of France and even supported he cardinal in his territorial ambitions. He was not afraid of Richelieu's gains in influence and did much to support and consolidate Richelieu's territorial influence- for example, in early 1626, he was appointed 'Grand maitre et surintendant general du commerce', whilst in January 1627 he gained the office of Admiral of France, previously held by Montmorency. Louis conferred upon Richelieu the right to a share of the proceeds of all shipwrecks, flotsam, jetsam and the confiscation of ships and merchandise at sea. He was allowed to take the proceeds of permits from French ships and in December 1628, he acquired a life annuity from French ports. Lastly, in February 1631, he was granted the power and responsibility to nominate all naval officers and in turn receive a stipend from said offices. Richelieu was wealthy- by the late 1630's the revenues earned by the Grand Maitre varied between 200,000 livres and 240,000 livres a year (cf. Knecht, Richelieu). In other words- to coin a phrase, Louis was perfectly relaxed for his cardinal to get filthy rich.

Personally, the cardinal kept a frugal life- a lesson he had probably learnt from his studies for the priesthood. He took his meals alone, being content with two courses per meal. After, he would relax. At Reuil, he would visit and take walks in the garden. He liked to listen to music, but devoted little time to such amusements. His preferred form of relaxation was conversation. He preferred the solitude and quietness of the countryside, rather than the hussle and bustle of Paris. He preferred the suburbs and enjoyed the quietness of Rueil. He was a loner and very much disliked giving audiences. Many found the cardinal intimidating- even aloof, though at times the cardinal let his guard down and could be 'affable and charming'. For example, after a military of campaign the people of Montauban whom he had defeated were surprised by his 'sweetness and modesty'. Richelieu impressed all with his intelligence. 'Reason', wrote the cardinal 'must be the universal rule and guide; all things must be done according to reason without allowing oneself to be swayed by emotion'. Richelieu was savvy and quick- he wrote numerous memos to the king signal his appreciation of state problems. He got to the heart of the matter balancing arguments for and against a particular decision. He left the king to make a final decision but offered is own preferred course of action, which the king was free to take on board or reject. Once he made a decision he stuck to it (cf. Knecht, Richelieu).

Despite achieving significant political powers, Richelieu did not forget the religious background that had formed him and had allowed him to acquire said political powers. As the historian, R.J Knecht, notes, his household and court was full of churchmen. He was very much dedicated to wellbeing of the church and made sure that they were well looked after by appointing many members of the church to positions of power and responsibility in the governance of France. Together they assisted the cardinal in his governance of France. All of his chamberlains became bishops, as did some of his confessors. The latter amongst others included Jacques Lescot, a theologian of repute who became a significant reforming prelate. Richelieu's close acquaintance, Father Joseph, a Capuchin monk was noted as a competent preacher, missionary, reformer and writer of several spiritual works. Later Richelieu was to use the latter later in his career as an agent during diplomatic negotiations (cf. Wedgwood). Doctrinally, Richelieu was orthodox and an ultramonatone- he had little time or truck with Jansenism of which he was one of the first opponents (cf. Knecht, Richelieu). In that sense, Richelieu was very much loyal and dedicated to the catholic church which he did much to contribute to its development and improvement.

Richelieu involved himself in the church's internal reformation- the counter reformation. In collaboration with the reformer, St Vincent de Paul he discussed the need to establish seminaries in order to improve the quality of the clergy. St Vincent opened a seminary in Paris 1642. He also persuaded the Oratorians to establish several seminaries. He diligently applied himself to the selecting worthy candidates for the role of bishops. As Knecht, notes this resulted in one of most talented set of bishops for France in a generation. He also applied himself to reforming orders such as the Benedictines and the Cistercians and sought to reform the medicant orders. For example, Du Plessis invited the Capuchins, a branch of the mendicant Franciscans to set up base in France- they established houses at la Sables d'Olonne in 1616 and in Lucon, Richelieu's seat in 1619 (cf. Levi, Cardinal Richelieu and the Making of France). Richelieu was enlightened- he cared for females and their position in the church. With his support, Father Joseph founded the nuns of Notre-Dame du Calvaire whose idea it was the king should dedicate France to the protection of the virgin Mary. He kept close contact with the Carmelites.

Richelieu as well as being a practical reformer, he was also an academic in his own right- he kept in constant contact with the academic world which had formed him. He found time to dedicate himself to the task of writing theological treatises, inspiring others to do the same (cf. Levi, Cardinal Richelieu and the Making of France). As his confessor noted, he 'devoted to this not only what remained to him of hours in the day, but also usually a great part of the night'. His writings as Knecht notes demonstrates 'a solid grounding in the Catholic faith' (cf. Knecht, Richelieu). For example the 78 page 'Briefve et facile instruction pour les confesseurs' 'organised round the decalouge and the commandments of the church, insist[ed] on the individual's obligations to God, church, prince and country.' It contains the bishop's own contribution to catholic thought. 'He recommends worship in the vernacular, is moderate on the Huguenots, but does not allow Catholic assistance at Huguenot ceremonies, mixed marriages, or ecclesiastic burial for heretics' (cf. Levi, Cardinal Richelieu and the Making of France). Despite his library containing works of the mystics such as St John of the Cross and St Theresa of Avila, Armand himself was not a mystic- '[h]e did not possess to any degree that sense of spiritual sinfulness that is so striking among the mystics, who were always so worried about the impurity brought by pride into the motives of the finest deeds'. He treated mystics with disdain- even contempt. He imprisoned the mystic, sending the abbe of St Cyran to prison at Vincennes in May 1638. Several chapters of Richelieu's work, unfinished 'Traite de la Perfection du Chretien' attacked the abbe- 'Contemplation', wrote the cardinal 'is far more liable to deceive than action…it is very dangerous in matters of faith to follow new paths, to have a particular devotion…. On this basis many do not think of themselves as truly devout unless they set up a new order'. Richelieu also made contribution to catholic doctrine where he made a special study of issues concerning contrition. For Richelieu as opposed to the jansenist preference for the elites to receive absolution, Richelieu was more concerned with the mental comprehension view, where he noted that as long as the penitent sought to avoid sin in the future, then all would be well (cf. Treasure, Cardinal Richelieu and the Development of Absolutism).

In his personal life, Richelieu was not particularly austere. He was the wealthiest and most powerful man in France- he did not wear a monks habit under his crimson red robes as was custom with men of his standing and position. He lived extravagantly. He bought land, houses and patronised and collected works of art. He kept a court, like the king, filled as it were with courtiers, secretaries, servants, soldiers and pages- they were his entourage, as such. Historians have tended to portray Richelieu as 'vain, faithless, arrogant, shy, vindictive, cruel, grasping, and much else besides' (cf. Knecht, Richelieu). That is not strictly true- Richelieu was an astonishingly competent and efficient minister- he knew what worked for France. Despite his enormous wealth and control of France, he never sought to threaten the king's position as supreme ruler of France- on the contrary, all tasks that he completed, he did for the greater glory of king and country.

CHAPTER 3

Richelieu and the nobility

In Richelieu's autobiographical 'Testament Politique', he promised to use the authority and responsibility offered to him by Louis to 'abase the pride of the nobles'. However according to Knecht, the cardinal was not that hostile to the nobles. Far from it- he was well aware of the role and importance of the nobility in governing France in concert with the king. Other parts of the 'Testament' praise the position and centrality of the nobility, crucial to the smooth functioning of the country. He called the nobility, 'the nerve of the state' and viewed the nobility as the backbone of the army. He cared, empathised and commiserated with the nobility over their own diminishing powers from the sale of offices to the new nouveau riche who were officers (cf. Knecht, Richelieu)- and did much to restore their previous powers and responsibilities.

Richelieu understood just what the nobility needed- after all he too was a nobleman given that he was a descendant of a minor noble family and was himself, in his own affairs, the epitome of kindness- even noblesse and a 'perfect example of aristocratic values' (cf. Knecht, Richelieu). Richelieu was very much supportive of the nobility- he granted them governorships, charged them with responsibility over military affairs and gifted them offices of court. He involved them in the decision making process that often befell a government. Richelieu held the nobility in high esteem- as a social climber he often married members of his own family into the families of members of the nobility. For example he arranged the marriage of his niece, Claire Clemence de Breze to the future 'Grand Conde' in 1641. In that sense Richelieu was well aware of the importance of the nobility to the functioning of France and even his own career- both personally and professionally- he treated the nobility with kindness and was considerate of their needs and requirements. He was well aware of their importance, their social prestige and their social advantage that such nobles would bring his family once he married members of his family to members of the nobility. Richelieu in that sense was a social climber, well aware of the lustre that the nobility brought him, in his association with them. Between the two- minister and nobility, there was mutual

Louis XIV and Richelieu

respect where each held the other in high esteem, Both minister and noble were necessary for the 'glory' of king and country. Both Richelieu and the nobility collaborated with each other to incarnate and make comprehensible the king's and for that matter- France's 'gloire'.

That is not to say that he was uncritical of the nobility- far from it- where there were areas that ill-suited the nobility – du Plessis did much to correct the nobles. He was adamant that the nobles should play an important part and a central role in the life of France. He also believed that they should refrain from all manners of political intrigue and should be loyal to the crown (cf. Knecht, Richelieu). In a sense Richelieu, more than any other leader, professionalised the nobility, sharpening them up and prepared them well for their role as the key collaborators with the king and his ministers. This model, created by Richelieu was to heavily influence the likes of Louis xiv and Richelieu's successor, Cardinal Mazarin who made extensive use of the nobles where he kept them at Versailles where he could have easy access to them, drawing on their ideas to inform his plans, polices and strategy for France.

According to the nobles, they were vassals and instruments of government rather than merely subjects- their service to the king was 'personal and voluntary'. The king shared in the substantive nature of the nobility and was 'primus inter pares'- that is to say, the first among equals. Both had mutual obligations buttressed by honour and fealty. Members of the nobility often attached themselves to others, in a bid to further their advancement. Some nobles at Louis' court attached themselves to the king's brother, Gaston d'orleans who involved his clients- members of the nobility in intrigue and scandal, plus several plots against Richelieu rebelling against his policies (cf. Knecht, Richelieu). The king and Richelieu were well aware of the lustre of grandeur that association with the members of the nobility brought them and did much to enhance and capitalise on said association.

Whenever the nobility strayed too far away from their duties as the king's helpers, Louis and Richelieu responded accordingly, corrected them and brought them back into line, reminding them of their responsibilities and loyalties to the crown and France- such was their closeness and mutual appreciation. For example, Richelieu checked the powers of the nobility by abolishing the position and role of Constable of France in 1626 and ordered all fortified castles to be abolished except those that needed to be defended against invaders (cf. Collins).

Louis and Richelieu sought to end duelling, a popular activity and pastime of the nobility. Duelling was a popular sport of the nobility, reaching its zenith in the

Louis XIV and Richelieu

sixteenth century. However, the activity soon fell out of favour. The Council of Trent condemned the practice, whilst various legislation was passed in France outlawed the practice but to no avail or effect. Personally, Richelieu was very much against the practice- he had his reasons. His father and his brother were involved in duelling accidents. The Edict of February 1626 imposed several penalties on the duellers. The duellers were treated harshly, leading Richelieu to commiserate: 'it is impossible for a noble heart not to feel sympathy for this young nobleman whose youth and courage evoked deep compassion'. But the cardinal was strengthened in his resolve to end the practice using the tools of the state to ban the practice. Richelieu's 'Memoires' leads one to conclude that the ban on duelling was successful. No duels were mentioned in the 'Mercure francois', for the following years after the fatality. However the ban and moratorium was not to last long- the next decade saw a revival in duelling. The king was frustrated and displeased at the prevalence of duelling in his land and kingdom- 'the abuse is once more getting the upper hand over the laws'. According to Knecht, Richelieu cannot take the credit for the eventual disappearance of duelling- it was a practice that continued well into the duration of his days of governorship (cf. Knecht, Richelieu).

In 1638, there was a new agent on the block- as it

were- the eighteen year old noble, Henri d'Effiat, Marquis de Cinq-Mars, who was the son of a friend of the cardinal who had previously been on the king's council. Cinq-Mars became the king's favourite, threatening to replace the cardinal in the king's affections. Cinq-Mars asked for a place on the king's inner council. Richelieu was opposed to Mar's growing influence and when Mars was caught up in a plot with the king's brother, Gaston d'Orleans, to have Richelieu assassinated, Richelieu learnt about the plot from his spies and duly took the opportunity to dispatch Mars- his rival on 12 September 1642. A few weeks later, Richelieu himself passed away (cf. Knecht, Richelieu, Sturdy, Richelieu and Mazarin).

After the Day of Dupes, which had confirmed Richelieu as de facto second in command of France, the cardinal took the opportunity to capitalise on his success by removing all opposition. This he did, with devastating ruthlessness. One of the key victims of the Day of Dupes was Marshal Louis de Marillac, who as commander of the French army based in Italy sought to invade France, Richelieu decided to deal with the threat by arresting the marshal and brought him back to France where he would be tried by a special court. The court was filled with judges, hand-picked by Richelieu himself, though when the judges found Marshal innocent, Richelieu convened another court based at his own house at Rueil- filled with his own supporters and 'creatures'. This time the court found Marshal guilty and was duly dispatched of.

Richelieu's actions concerning the fate of Marshal was met with hostility and disapproval. Chanteloube, one of the Queen Mother's pamphleteers summised the general gist of dissension:

'To-day it is generally accepted that it is just to imprison anyone because of the slightest wish of a favourite (for all know that these acts do not come from the king). Every suspicion is cause for imprisonment; every imprisonment is authorised by the judges. Every pretext is a crime; every crime is subject to condemnation; every condemnation is for not less than life. Whoever displeases a favourite is put in prison, and whoever is in prison must be executed to justify the act of him who caused him to be imprisoned'.

One could argue that Richelieu was justified in his reaction to the Marshal affair. What else could he do- Marshal had attacked France for no good reason- Marshal had to be dealt with accordingly.

Richelieu had another dispute with the nobility in his dealings with Henri duc de Montmorency, a prince of the blood- that is to say- a cousin of the king. Montmorency belonged to one of the high ranking noble families – as well as being a prince of the blood, he was also Henry iv's godson and brother in law to the prince of Conde. Montmorency was governor of Languedoc.

There was an internal dispute when Richelieu sought to impose taxation in Languedoc- the elus. Montmorency after initially agreeing to the policy, then backtracked after being convinced by the bishop of Ali ad other local supporters to oppose the cardinal's plans. Montmorency was widely supported- he had many intercessors who sought to rescue him- a crowd gathered, shouting 'Pardon him, pardon him, have mercy on him'. The king would not listen, supporting and siding with Richelieu: 'No pardon shall be granted him'. Montmorency was duly dispatched of (cf. Knecht, Richelieu). This was arguably an overreaction- Montmorency was a popular figure in France, well admired and held in high esteem- what could he do but defend and protect his vicinity.

France soon entered a military dispute with Spain in May 1635. This caused Richelieu to keep tabs on the activities of the nobility. Any members of the nobility who sided with Spain were accordingly dealt with. One of Richelieu's first victims was Louis Clausel, commander of the French forces in the Valtelline who supported Spain. He was condemned in October 1635 and was dispatched of in November. Another member of the nobility, Adrien de Monduc, comte de Cramail, was dealt with in a similarly harsh manner. After expressing his view that France should back out of the war, Richelieu threw him into the Bastille on Spain May 1638.

Louis XIV and Richelieu

The relationship between Richelieu and the nobility is somewhat complex. The cardinal could at times be incredibly kind and even empathetic and sympathetic to their needs- after all he too was a nobleman- he understood and he got them. At other times, he could be harsh- even cruel to them. That is one interpretation. The other is that Richelieu dealt with nobility in a manner of fairness. Where they erred, he duly corrected them- where they acted correctly he was not afraid to praise and reward them accordingly. For the most part, he treated them with kindness and civility- after all, he too was a member of the minor nobility- something of which he was well aware of and even proud of. Hence one could note that Richelieu and the nobility engaged themselves in a battle of friendly rivalry- each causing the other to raise their game accordingly.

Of course such was Richelieu's success with the nobility that it spectacularly backfired on him where the nobles during the reign of Louis' successor- Louis' son, the dauphin, Louis xiv suffered a revolt from the nobles- twice, which is known as the Frondes. The nobles enjoyed such a power and a prestige under Richelieu, that when said powers and prestige was attacked by the absolutist regency during Louis' xiv's times they sought to once again, reclaim their position as the leading faction and group in France during the Frondes by rebelling against the king and dauphin. The Frondes came to a successful ending when the nobles were once again reconciled to the king and in the process reverted back to their role of governing France in collaboration with the King.

CHAPTER 4

Richelieu and the Huguenots

France religion wise, was divided and disunited. The dispute between Catholics and Protestant Huguenots was a headache for Louis and his cardinal. Louis was Roman Catholic and took his title of 'Most Christian King' very seriously and with much pride. Louis adopted the governing accompanying principle of the 'divine right of kings' seriously- as king, he was God's first and chief representative on earth, sent from heaven above to cure France of all her ills and worries. According to Louis, he had the 'king's touch' which granted him miraculous healing powers which he used to improve the health of all those who came into contact with him. Louis very much wanted to convert the Huguenots to Catholicism, creating in France 'one king, one law, one faith' (cf. Knecht, Richelieu). Louis was ambitious for his country- he wanted to secure France as the leading Roman Catholic country. However, in a stroke of enlightened thought he refused to revoke the Edict of Nantes, which gave the Huguenots a set of rights and freedom to practice their religion freely without fear of prosecution- or even persecution- in that sense, Louis was a moderate and sensible catholic in the Salesian tradition.

The most serious domestic issue which confronted Richelieu was another rebellion by the protestant Huguenots. Although at Montpellier, peace had been established between the crown and the Huguenots, those in La Rochelle, did not fully support the crown and were suspicious of Richelieu's intentions. They had economic as well as religious fears (cf. Sturdy, Richelieu and Mazarin).

Richelieu took a keen interest in the economic revival of France, to which he expanded maritime and commercial concerns. He also created overseas trading companies rivalling the likes of such companies in both Holland and England.

In 1626, when Richelieu was appointed 'Grand Maitre de la Navigation et du commerce', an office which granted him powers over the administration of colonies, he set out to embark on his new position with relish. In 1625 he presented to the king a 'reglement pour la mer' in which he called for the expansion of the mediterranean fleet to protect French shipping and to secure access to northern Italy by sea. Richelieu lent his support to the establishment of trading companies such as the 'Compagnie du Morbihan' (or Compagnie des Cent Associes, as it became known) was founded to trade in the West Indies and Canada, and also the Compagnie de Saint-Pierre which sought to trade with Canada. Richelieu had high hopes for French interests in North America in the 'Compagnie de la Nouvelle France (1628): it would not only conduct trade in North America, but he also sought to establish colonies, transport emigrants, oversee the construction of towns and ports and generally advance the interests of France in their part of the world (cf. Sturdy, Richelieu and Mazarin).

Richelieu was at the zenith of his powers, teaming with ideas. His attention turned to the war fleet. Plans were made to extend French military presence to serve the North Sea and Atlantic as well as the Mediterranean. Whilst such an expansion was greeted with approval in areas such as Paris, areas such as Saint Malo and La Rochelle felt threatened by the expansion, where their merchant communities and municipal authorities saw the expansion as dangerous to their trading patterns and hence their prosperity (cf. Sturdy, Richelieu and Mazarin).

The Spanish, Dutch and English governments followed Richelieu's plans with much interest. The English in a pre-emptive strike in order to check the cardinal's maritime ambitions. In 1637, the duc de soubise, a Huguenot military leader, was in exile in England when he appealed to Charles I of England to send military help to the Huguenots of La Rochelle, to secure and protect their liberties. Charles in defence of the Huguenots, attacked and invaded La Rochelle (cf. Sturdy, Richelieu and Mazarin).

Louis and Richelieu convened an army of some 20,000 and laid siege to the city. The campaign was a success. On 29 October 1628 La Rochelle surrendered to the king. On 1 November, Louis entered the city. It was decided that the Huguenots should retain rights of worship, although the practice of Catholicism was quickly restored to the city (cf. Sturdy, Richelieu and Mazarin).

As news of the recapturing of La Rochelle spread, messages of congratulations poured in from many parts of England. Their reputation reached heights that had previously eluded them. The two men- Louis and Richelieu bonded over their joint enterprise in La Rochelle- they enjoyed a closeness that had previously escaped them. Rights were granted to the Huguenots where they had rights to practice their religion without further interference from other institutions (cf. Sturdy, Richelieu and Mazarin).

Events were not over- far from it. The following year, whilst the siege of La Rochelle was progressing, Soubise's brother, the duc de Rohan gathered an army and occupied Nimes, Montauban, Castres and other towns. Against this offence, the crown dispatched the Prince of Conde and Duc de Montmorency. In 1628 both sides lost many people. The war continued until both sides decided to settle for peace. The resulting 'Peace of Alais', guaranteed full rights of worship to all Huguenot towns which recognised the king's authority. The Huguenots agreed for their fortifications to be dismantled as a guarantee that they would not rebel again. Despite this setback, most if not all of the privileges that the Huguenots had secured from the 'Edict of Nantes' was once again affirmed, though they lost their political rights and protections. Both sides reconciled with one another- no hard feelings involved- even the chief instigator- Rohan was dealt with kindness- he was later appointed as head of the French army (cf. Sturdy, Richelieu and Mazarin).

CHAPTER 5

Foreign Policy

Richelieu as first minister was tasked with the issue of dealing with the relationship between France and her European partners. He sought to achieve 'glory' for the king by asserting France as a global player and a leading country in the continent of Europe. Richelieu was very much a realpolitik- in his 'Testament politique' he noted the need for realpolitik and continuous pragmatic diplomacy: 'it is absolutely necessary', he writes, 'for the well-being of the state to negotiate ceaselessly, either openly or secretly, and in all places, even in those from which no future prospects as yet seem likely' (cf. Knecht, Richelieu). For the most part, Richelieu of France was engaged in a battle with the powerful Spanish and Austrian House of Hapsburg family. Most of his policies concerning foreign affairs was 'anti-Hapsburg' in essence and substance where he sought to check and frustrate their growing powers and influence.

According to the historian, Herman Weber, Richelieu sought to achieve peace in Europe and peace in Christendom, but failed to achieve said peace. According to Weber disputes in Europe occurred can be attributed to the actions of the crown- Richelieu included. As Dickman notes, 'whether tragic or guilty', 'the effect of Richelieu's policies of peace, they were fatal to peace itself (cf. Bergin, Brockliss, Richelieu and his Age). Whilst I accept that Richelieu desired to achieve peace he was not a passive but sought a proactive and active foreign policy in order to achieve peace- even military campaigns were used to achieve said peace (cf. Bergin, Brockliss, Richelieu and his Age).

The illustrious Hapsburg family enjoyed presence in their Austrian and Spanish branches, achieving much success in their respective territories. The Thirty Years War began as a result of a war of proxy between France and the Spanish Hapsburg when France supported Holland over Spanish aggression via the 'Treaty of Compiegne in June 1624 (cf. Moote, Louis xiii, the Just).

In the war, concerning Spain and the Dutch Republic, the Dutch achieved success by liberating provinces from Spanish control in the mid-1620's, and by 1679 Dutch borders were relatively secure, though the Spanish threat was not completely over. The war seeped and shaded into the Thirty Years War. France despite its alliance with the Dutch, in which Richelieu agreed with a protestant army general Mansfield to receive French subsidies to attack the Spanish in the Palatinate. Hence there was a war of proxy and a cold war between France and Spain. The Hapsburgs were enjoying territorial success, whilst France was withering. The Treaty of Moncon signed between France and Spain which caused a ceasefire, soon ceased until the Mantuan affair (cf. Moote, Sturdy, Richelieu and Mazarin).

Shortly after being appointed first minister, Richelieu was faced with a crisis in Valtellina, a valley in Lombard (northern Italy). The Valtellina was a strip of land between Milan, the Spanish stronghold and Austria. Its inhabitants were predominantly Catholic though they were ruled by protestants, known as the Grey League or Grisons- if you will. In 1620 the Spanish Hapsburg family invaded the territory in order to free its inhabitants from protestant rule. They expelled the Grisons and installed a catholic government. Venice, Savoy, Mantua as well as the German states became worried at the increasing influence of Spain on the continent (cf. Sturdy, Richelieu and Mazarin). Despite being catholic, Richelieu failed to support the catholic Hapsburgs family in their endeavours, despite being catholic and heading Catholic France, probably to check the growing power of the Hapsburgs. Instead, in an act of devastating and ruthless realpolitiking he supported the Protestant Swiss canton of Grisons, who had claims to the valley. Armand sent troops to Valtellina where the Pope's troops were driven out (cf. Wedgewood). Richelieu had a good, confident and assured debut and start.

The second war and dispute concerned the Mantuan war of succession- or the Mantuan affair- if you will. Vincenzo II, passed away- he was the last member of the House of Gonzaga and ruler of the duchies of Mantua and Montferrat. The territories consisted of the Spanish road, a passage which allowed Spanish supplies to be carried over from Italian territory. The result of the death of Vicenzo was a proxy war between France who supported the French-born Duke of Nevers, and Spain, who supported his cousin the Duke of Guastalia. Fighting was concentrated mainly in the fortress of Casale in Montferrat, which Spain besieged twice from March 1628 to April 1629, then September 1629 to October 1630. French intervention in support of Nevers in April 1629 led to the transfer of Imperial troops from Northern Germany to support Spain. Despite taking Mantua in July 1630, the French backed Swedish Intervention in the Thirty Years War forced Emperor Ferdinand II to withdraw his troops and make peace.

The Treaty of Cherasco confirmed the French backed

Nevers as Duke of Mantua and Montferrat, in return for minor territorial losses. More significantly, it left the French in possession of Pinerolo and Casale, which controlled access to passes through the Alps. The French led by Louis and Richelieu had succeeded. France was a successful global power situated in Europe. Perhaps the greatest legacy of Richelieu is his establishment of France as a dominant and well respected player on the global scene.

Richelieu's third war was the Swedish affair. Richelieu in his anti-Hapsburg policy, then set himself the task of purging Italy and Germany of the Austrian side of the Hapsburg family. As he told the German Electors, Louis xiii was 'driven by a very sincere desire to free Italy and Germany from the oppression to which they had been reduced by the manifest violence and ambition of the House of Austria'. After invading Germany in her bid to liberate her from Hapsburg presence, the Swedish monarch, Gustavus Adolphus intervened in a bid to unite the protestant faction. Although on friendly terms with Sweden, Richelieu did not support Gustavus' intervention because it prevented Father Joseph's wish to negotiate between protestant and catholic princes. It was now Gustavus and not Louis who viewed as the saviour and liberator of Germany. When Gustavus passed away, this event did much to put Richelieu foreign politicking back on course, now that Gustavus was out of the way. France made a treaty with Sweden where Sweden was free to 'desert France at any time'. Sweden was allowed to keep control of 'Mainz and Worms' (Knecht, Richelieu).

It is generally agreed amongst historians that Richelieu did much to improve France's military forces. There was a significant increase in the number of troops whilst civilian presence was increased. Army numbers grew in July 1635 to a total of 160,000 men (134,000 infantry; 26,000 cavalry). He also sought to improve the treatment that members of the army received- for example he improved the deliveries of bread and forage to the army (cf. Knecht, Richelieu)- keeping them well fed as it were hence preparing them for times of war and battles. With Richelieu, the military flourished, becoming more efficient and more effective now that it was populated with men of high quality and calibre- they never looked back.

Richelieu's foreign policy was driven by hard headedness and a ruthless pragmatism- in that sense, he was not ideological but was a pragmatist. Richelieu was a successful diplomat who skilfully negotiated his way out of trouble and problems. In that sense Richelieu influenced the likes of the realpoltick American politician Henry Kissenger. He was ambitious for both king and country and sought to enforce the policy of 'gloire' for both king and France.

CHAPTER 6

Domestics

Richelieu is credited with devising the political method and style of monarchical absolutism which was to influence generations of monarchs of France reaching its apogee in the times of Louis xiv- that is to say royal sovereignty and power were exclusive upon which no body and person could overturn or even challenge the sovereign's decisions and policies (cf. Sturdy, Richelieu and Mazarin). According to Knecht, that is not strictly true. According to Knecht, the theory of absolutism can be traced back to roman times- it did not begin in Richelieu's times but stretched further back in time: in the third century Ulpian coined the maxim: 'what pleases the prince has the force of law'. The idea of a king having supreme control of his land, dates back to the fifteenth century when the maxim was given credence in France. Despite the term 'absolutism' stretches back to the French revolution, the maxim 'absolute power' actually hails from the medieval ages (cf. Knecht Richelieu, Bonney, 'Absolutism, What's in a name', French History, L'Absolutisme). As for the practice of absolutism Knecht notes that such a practice was developed before Richelieu's times where in sixteenth century France, royal authority was asserted and could not be overturned by an individual or an institution. Whereas such a practice dovetailed with the principle of the 'divine right of king's' where the crown had supreme authority legitimated and granted to him by god, Richelieu according to Knecht ushered and implemented a more secular form of the theory of absolutism (cf. Knecht, Richelieu).

Richelieu was encouraged by the king to increase the government's finances in order to support France's foreign adventures as well as funding the French army and fleets. Richelieu left the task and administration of collating taxes and revenues to the surintendants and intendants who worked out the finer details of accounting. However Richelieu and the king maintained for themselves the financial strategy and trajectory that France would take before delegating responsibility to the surintendants (cf. Sturdy, Richelieu and Mazarin) who duly carried out their appointed tasks.

For Richelieu, the main strategy was to increase the

revenue and other forms of income. France was at war with Spain. Financially, France could not compete- Spain had streams of income from her vast territories such as Spanish America, the Spanish Netherlands, Portugal, southern Italy and Sicily, in addition to the income of Spain itself. France was out of its depth- she had a smaller pool of income- he had to rely upon French domestic resources supplemented by loans from other countries (cf. Sturdy, Richelieu and Mazarin). Once France entered the Thirty Years War, military expenditure rose by a significant amount. From an average of less than 16 million livres a year in the 1620s to over 33 million after 1635 and over 38 million after 1640. In essence the crown should have able to meet these expenses since the government's revenue and income totalled at an estimated 108 million. However in reality the amount actually collated was less than the official figure. As France was drawn into war, Richelieu and his fellow ministers embarked on what were unpopular fiscal policies, which cause domestic unrest at home.

Politically, Richelieu was an authoritarian- even an absolutist. He used the model and system of surintendants and intendants to supervise France. The system of the intendants has its heritage in the middle ages. The system underwent different incarnations before settling in its present form by the time of Richelieu. By 1624, when the cardinal became first minister, the role of intendants performed an advisory or supervisory function. Originally they were not that numerous- between 1560 and 1630, only about 120 were appointed, and in 1624 there were only seven working in the provinces (cf. Sturdy, Richelieu and Mazarin).

During his first few years, Richelieu did little to disturb the numbers of intendants, but after the Day of Dupes, where he learnt the lesson that he should keep a tight leash on the country in order to prevent further rebellion and further displeasure from Louis. Richelieu raised his game- he increased the number of intendants- between 1630 and 1648, approximately 120 and 150 intendants were appointed, respectively. According to Sturdy, Richelieu was driven to increase the intendants not because it dovetailed with his philosophy of government (in his Political Testament, he had expressed disdain at the use of commissioners such as the intendants), but because he was driven by circumstances. That is correct- as a conservative, Richelieu adapted with ease to the demands of the times- he was not an ideologue barred and bounded by ideology- but was a pragmatist in the sense that he responded to the evidence and facts of the situation as he saw fit, rather than allying himself to a strict and absolute theory. The increase in France's international commitments coupled with domestic trouble at home, left Richelieu with little

Louis XIV and Richelieu

option but to increase the number of intendants by the early 1640s where they were sent to all of the provinces in a bid to improve the collation of taxes and in order to quell rebellion. Together they were the eyes and ears of the government (cf. Sturdy, Richelieu and Mazarin, Campbell, Louis xiv).

According to the historian, Richard Bonney, there were three main taxes that the government collected. There were direct taxes, indirect taxes, and affaires extraordinaires. The taille and Taillon were direct taxes. Prior to Richelieu's times, the collation of taxation was privatised but brought back under state control by Richeliue's time including other new taxes such as the new military tax- the subsistances. Government income was also fortressed by loans from financiers and wealthy individuals. Indirect taxes such as the gabelles, a salt on tax was abolished. The third tax was the 'affaires extroadinairres' which was other taxes that did not fall under the previous two taxes. The extraordinary taxes were raised by the method of the 'traites'- that is to say, one-off contracts with financiers and wealthy individuals. The financier 'undertook to raise a fixed sum of money in return for a standard rate of interest' (cf. Bergin, Brockliss, Richelieu and his Age). In a sense the extraordinary taxes were like bonds where government receives loans in return for a promise that said government will pay and refund loans with added interest.

According to Knecht, the yield from both direct and indirect taxes was insufficient to fund and finance the governments wartime expenses. As a result, the government relied on extraordinary taxes to fund its activities (cf. Knecht, Richelieu).

Richelieu and Louis appointed only five surintendents who assisted them in the collation of revenue. They included: Bochart de Champigny, Marilllac, d'Ettiat, and Buillon and Bouthillier, the last two of whom served for a total of just over eight years (cf. Bergin, Brockliss, Richelieu and his Age). The last two were responsible for raising funds for Louis' and Richelieu' foreign adventures (cf. Knecht, Richelieu). For the best part the surintendants were given freedom by Richelieu and Louis where they had the discretion to do as they saw fit with regards to the collation of taxes. For example in 1635 Richelieu wrote to Bullion:

'I fully admit my ignorance of financial matters and realise that you are so well-versed in the subject that the only advice I can give you is to make use of those whom you find most useful to the king's service, and to rest assured that I will second you in every way I can' (cf. Knecht, Richelieu). Bullion's task was difficult, nigh on impossible. Although the king's revenues had increased since 1630 from 48 million livres to nearly 57.5 million, the amount received by the Treasury was far less than anticipated (cf. Knecht, Richelieu).

According to Sturdy, by the early 1630s, the government only received 25 percent of the taille- the rest was stolen by the local financial officers. In 1634 Richelieu set up a commission to investigate the problem as to why the revenue wasn't filtering through to the government. In response to the commission, Richelieu set out to reform the system. Officiers, rather receiving a stream of income, would now be paid in bonds, the number of people exempt from paying the taille was reduced hence broadening the tax and revue base, plus the numbers and powers of the intendants was increased in order to monitor the officers. All of these reforms were designed to ensure that the financiers stuck to their role without being corrupt. The intendants were issued with instructions in 1634. They were sent to the generalites, where they interviewed the officiers in order to identify the major abuses in the collection of the taille, but it was left to the intendants to correct said abuse. Overall, the intendants sought to improve the collection of the taille- making its collection more efficient (cf. Sturdy, Richelieu and Mazarin).

The intendants also exercised juridical duties- for example they punished the leaders of rebellions and 'conducted investigations into the conduct of nobles, magistrates and others suspected of being implicated in sedition'. They also prepared cases against the aforementioned, even presiding over said trails themselves. According to Sturdy Richelieu viewed the intendants as a short term and temporary measure- they were 'an extraordinary response to extraordinary circumstances' (cf. Sturdy, Richelieu and Mazarin). That is not strictly true- though the intendants were originally viewed as a short term measure- they soon proved useful as agents of the kingdom and proved valuable allies of the French government. They were very much a presence after the times of Richelieu continuing with leadership of Louis xiv, Louis' son and Cardinal Mazarin, Richelieu's successor.

Richelieu was enlightened- even a democrat. He left the parlementes to function with relative freedom. The parlementes, like the provincial Estates, enacted royal legislation and possessed the power to invalidate legislation. The senior parlement was based in Paris, the capital. Relations between crown and the Parlemente of Paris were cordial. The Parlemente regarded itself as the supreme and leading authority in France, though this was never acknowledged by the crown. According to members of the Parlemente, they were the ones who successfully navigated and steered France through the trauma of the wars of religion. In more recent times,

Louis XIV and Richelieu

it was the Parlemente that recognised the regency of Marie de Medici following the assassination of Henry iv, thereby preventing any further dispute as to whom should govern France. Though Richelieu often clashed with the parlementes over matters of policy he recognised its authority and never questioned it's role as a judicial institution- he had no desire to carry out major reforms to the parlementes and respected their sphere of influence (cf. Sturdy, Richelieu and Mazarin).

Richelieu was often met with opposition from the parlementes regarding fundraising for the crown's activities. In 1629, in order to speed up the process and streamline the process of enacting laws, Richelieu sought to make the parlementes more efficient. He enacted the Code Michau, which was overseen by Marillac, which noted that parlemente had two months to enact legislation otherwise failure to register said legislation within two months would be registered and enacted automatically. The Code anticipated the practice that the liberal party and government introduced in Britain with the Parliament Act which granted the House of Commons more powers and reduced the powers of the House of Lords when matters came to the enactment and legitimation of statutes. In 1631, Louis passed an Edict which barred parlemente from discussing legislation that was political in nature. Louis' actions were caused by parlemente's refusal to side with Louis over his dispute with Gaston d'Orleans. This was a significant curtailment and curbing of parlemente's powers (cf. Sturdy, Richelieu and Mazarin). Louis' actions were arguably an overreaction- his emasculation of parelmente's powers was to have serious repercussions later on in France's life, causing the French revolution where parlemente supported by the revolutionairres in overthrowing the king and queen in a bid to recover their lost powers caused by Louis.

There was often friction between the crown and the parlementes (cf. Knecht, Richelieu) hence causing Richelieu to respond with policies of his own designed to deal with the problems between the crown and parlemente. The friction was nothing new and had been ongoing for the best past of a century. For example, Francis I prevented the court from interfering in matters of state. With Louis xiii, the same policy was followed and adopted by the Keeper of the Seals, Michel de Marilac: Marilac informed the magistrates that their duty was judicial and not political (cf. Knecht, Richelieu). Richelieu embarked on more reforms to parlemente. Richelieu was also an authoritarian- he did all in his powers to curb the influence of the parlementes. For example when the parlementes failed to register the edict setting up the Chambre de l'Arsenal, a group of magistrates appeared before the king at Metz: 'You are here', said the king 'only to judge master Peter and master John, and I intend to keep you in your place; if you continue your machinations, I will cut your nails to the quick' (cf. Knecht, Richelieu). Richelieu often resorted to the system of 'lit de justice'. This was a system where the king visited parlemente and registered laws himself in collaboration with parlemente. Before the sixteenth century 'lits' were frequently called in order to incarnate unity between crown and parlemente. During and after the wars of religion, 'lits' were called in order to negotiate relations between crown and parlemente which were often strained. By the seventeenth century, 'lits' were ceremonies where the king visited his own parlemente in an act of unity and union. A lit de justice was often used to impose the king's will- for example, in 1635, a lit de justice was called when the crown sought to create new offices to be sold, including twenty-four in the Parlemente of Paris. Though Parlemente rejected the king's policy was enforced by the lit de justice. This policy was met with much dissent and opposition, causing judges and magistrates to go on strike. Richelieu responded to reduce the number of offices from twenty-four to seventeen. The final lit de justice that Richelieu enforced was in 1641 by which Parlement was barred from involving itself in political affairs of state (cf. Sturdy, Richelieu and Mazarin).

Richelieu also set himself the task of rooting out 'false [and ghost] nobles'- that is to say agents who were not nobles but were claiming exemption as nobles from the payment of taxes such as the 'taille'. In a bid to increase the crown's revenue Richelieu sought to make collection of the taille more efficient and more effective by sending the intendents across France to root out false nobles. For example, Richelieu sent out one force to Normandy in 1634 which examined the status of almost a thousand families- only 11 percent were claiming exemption. On closer examination, it turned out that they were all poor. The false nobles were placed on the 'taille rolls, but almost all were assessed at 10 livres, while a few years were so impecunious that they were assessed at zero'. Richelieu's strategy had spectacularly backfired- he had expected his tax base to significantly increase and widen- yet this proved not to be the case- false nobles existed of course, but their numbers were small- not enough to substantiate such a heavy handed policy (cf. Sturdy, Richelieu and Mazarin). Richelieu had initially believed that the false nobles could afford to pay the taille, however it soon proved that they were not that rich in the first place, to the point that they were too poor to pay any form of taxation.

As for the crown's revenue, Richelieu proved incompetent- one historian estimates that the government ran up annual deficits throughout the seventeenth century (approaching a balance in 1688), and that in the times of 1625 to 1633, the deficit ranged between 21,532,400 and 38,214,500 livres a year. As Sturdy notes, the crown ran up 'colossal debts'- that is the state of affairs, that Mazarin inherited from his predecessor Richelieu (cf. Sturdy, Richelieu and Mazarin).

Richelieu faced many rebellions from people who disagreed with his fiscal policy. Such rebellions were swiftly dealt with by Richelieu. For example, in November, soldiers were sent to occupy Caen, Avranches and scattered the Nu-pied army. Richelieu was ruthless- he sent the army across France to deal with the rebels- '[a]bout fifty were executed', seventy were imprisoned, and about forty were banished from Normandy, never to return again.

CHAPTER 7

Richelieu as Patron

As well as politics and economics, Richelieu's time in office was widely concerned with the patronage of the arts, letters and scholarship, both as a result of personal interest as well as the demands of statecraft. For Richelieu, the pen was a sword- the pen had the power to influence all manners of activities in France- the sword had the means to influence the people of France with astonishing ease. In this sense Richelieu anticipated the enlightenment and its celebration of the agency of human reason and human endeavour (cf. Sturdy, Richelieu and Mazarin).

Richelieu ascent to power coincides with the time when there was a rivalry between the humanists and the modernists. The humanists were mainly parliamentaires, magistrates and clergy who were influenced and looked back to the greco-roman authors for inspiration in their own works. For the modernists, they rejected the humanist support for Greco-roman authors and rejected said school as an authority. Writing in 1623, Theophile de Viau poured scorn on the use of the classic authors. Art he argued 'needed to be clear, direct and significant'. It was in the midst of this debate, that Richelieu founded the Academie Francaise in 1634.

Richelieu lived in an age when the power of the printing press was being realised and its ability to influence 'public opinion'. Richelieu himself adopted the maxim- 'gouverner, c'est faire croire' (in order to govern he had to make his guiding principles believable). According to Richelieu, he believed that the high culture of his day could be a powerful and efficient pollical ally (cf. Sturdy, Richelieu and Mazarin) in terms of improving the intellectual and cultural life of France. He began to deal with the cultural pastimes of the people of France- such was the growing sphere of influence over the personal lives of the French (cf. Sturdy, Richelieu and Mazarin.

As the historian Edric Caldicott, notes, Richelieu's art policy is filled with contradiction. He has been praised and condemned in equal measure for his involvement in France's cultural life: 'condemned for self-aggrandizement, but praised for enhancing the authority of the king; accused of introducing forms of censorship, but lauded for bringing order into the intellectual and artistic periphery

Louis XIV and Richelieu

of the monarchy' (cf. Bergin, Brockliss, Richelieu and his Age).

As Deloche points out, Richelieu trusted artists to make the correct decisions concerning works of art and delegated responsibility to the acquisition of works of arts to his few 'creatures' (cf. Bergin, Brockliss, Richelieu and his Age, Sturdy, Richelieu and Mazarin). That is not strictly true- whilst I accept that Richelieu delegated matters to others, he always kept abreast of developments- nothing was sanctioned without the cardinal's input and eventual approval.

In 1622, Richelieu was appointed principal of the Sorbonne- or rather the University of Paris as it is generally known (cf. Pitte). He presided over the renovation and improvement of the university buildings and oversaw the construction of its now famous chapel, making it more conducive for the use of students and lecturers.

Richelieu used the printing press as much as he used government and administration to fight his policy battles. He patronised writers and other scholars who could help him in publicising his strategy. Among those whom he patronised were Mathieu Morgues (the Abbe de Saint Germain), Jean Baudon, Scipion Dupleix and John Sirmond. These in tandem with other writers sought to write laudatory pamphlets and other publications applauding Richelieu's policies, praising his statecraft and waxed lyrical on his services to France. In some cases, writers wrote works flattering the cardinal in order to secure his patronage and support. One such figure was Jean Louis-Guez de Balzac. In Le Prince (1631), Balzac defended the cardinal against accusations of tyranny, and argued that his principle of 'raison d'etat' was a perfectly acceptable and legitimate principle of government. 'Reason of State' was in other words and effects, 'prudence', that is to say that Richelieu had the power to launch pre-emptive strikes on those who sought to cause trouble to France. It was better to punish those in anticipation of their actions rather than waiting after the action, by which it was too late- damage to the state had been done. According to Balzac, justice comes into force after a crime, 'prudence', 'prevents a crime or rebellion in the first place and should be employed by Richelieu unsparingly' (cf. Sturdy, Richelieu and Mazarin).

Richelieu was very much an academic and continued the academic practice of studying and writing. He kept in touch with the academic world where he founded two journals and periodicals: the 'Mercure Francois' and the 'Gazette' which kept him in touch with and abreast of the academic and intellectual life of France. The first, 'Mercure' was founded in 1603 as a yearly review of political and social events. In1624, Richelieu's friend and advisor Pere Joseph took up editorship of the periodical. Pere Joseph, as editor often published articles criticising the cardinal, but often also included rebuttals hence maintaining a freedom of speech and a balance, respectively. The 'Gazette' was founded by Theophraste Renaudot, who had come to the attention of Pere Joseph as a talented publicist. Renaudot hailed from the same part of France as Richelieu and was a contemporary of Richelieu where he was about the same age as Armand. He was well travelled, visiting Italy, the Netherlands and Germany. When he returned to Paris he set up a free medical clinic and organised events designed to discuss the political issues of the day. The 'Gazette' which he had founded with Richelieu's backing and support in 1631 contained news and comment, but also stuck to the government's line of message (cf. Sturdy, Richelieu and Mazarin).

Richelieu was very much a creative in his own right. He was dedicated to the task of ensuring that the arts and humanities flourished in France. He built theatres- at least two- of which one was based in Rueil, his ancestral home. These theatres according to Anthony Levi hosted 'court entertainments, ballets, court ballets, comedies lyriques, or comedie-ballets' The first smaller theatre was completed in about February 1636, whilst the larger was built and designed by Le Mercier having space for three hundred spectators. The latter was inaugurated with the performance of 'Mirame'. Richelieu was supported in his endeavours by the king and the queen, Louis xiii and his wife, Anne of Austria who attended the performance of 'Mirame' on 14 January. They also attended the ceremony held in 1641 to celebrate the marriage of Richelieu's niece, Claire Clemence de Maille-Breze to the duc d'Enghien, later known as the grand Conde, and at the time of performance, fifth in line to the throne (cf. Levi, Cardinal Richelieu and the Making of France). The 'Cinq Auteurs'- a group founded by the cardinal, composed three plays including, 'La Comedie des Tuileries (1635), La Grande Pastorale (1637), and L'Aveugle de Smyne (1637). It is generally known that Richelieu provided the outline plot and skeleton for the plays. Pelliston goes as far as to note that Richelieu wrote five hundred lines of 'La Grande Pastorale', 'a play never published and now lost' (cf. Bergin, Brockliss, Richelieu and his Age). He also chose cherry picked a set of five authors whom he could collaborate with- 'only two, Rotrou and Pierre Corneille, were primary authors of straight scripted drama' The rest were ether poets or authors of libretti (cf. Levi, Cardinal Richelieu and the Making of France).

Richelieu was also a writer in his own right. In that sense he maintained links with the academic world that had formed and shaped his intellect and character. He wrote many political and religious treatises. This included the 'Testament Politique' which outlined Richelieu's ideas on state governance. Du Plessis as well as being a commentor on the state was also of man of deep religious conviction. He authored the 'Instruction du chretien' a catechism that set out the principles and doctrine of the catholic church. As Bergin notes the catechism was popular and was widely distributed throughout France (cf. Bergin, The Rise of Richelieu). It became the standard text and point of reference for those who wanted to acquaint themselves with the standard doctrine of the church. As Knecht notes, Richelieu was one of the first ministers to commission memoranda and reports which could be used to inform ideas for policies (cf. Knecht, Richelieu), Richelieu anticipated modern day politics where leaders tend to commission think tanks and policy institutes as well as their internal researchers to advise on matters and affairs of state. After the Day of Dupes, Richelieu set himself the task of being the 'school master of the French people'. As well as being a writer, the cardinal surrounded himself with other writers at court. This group included Boisrobert, Paul Hay du Chastelet and Jean Chaperlain. Boisrobert after serving as avocat in the Parlement of Rouen, assumed the role of a court poet and was a sort of literary agent for the cardinal. He also played a leading role in the establishment of the Academy Francaise. Hay du Cahstelet, like Boisrober, an ex parliamentairre was regularly employed by Richelieu as spokesman to deal with the cardinal's critics. He too was a founder member of the Academy. Chapelain succeeded Boisrobert as official poet. He was devoted to Richelieu, calling him 'this divine man'. After 1630, this disparate group of men became members of the Academie Francaise and contributed to the cardinal's journal, the 'Gazette'.

As well as governing his own propaganda, Richelieu set out to deal with hostile commentators who did not favour his policies. Of course the press was controlled-printers needed licences to operate, and the Chancellor of France took measures to ensure that books, pamphlets and other materials complied and stayed within the bounds of the law. In 1623, Richelieu took the initiative of tightening up censorship where the Sorbonne was tasked with providing most of the censors. All books, pamphlets and materials had to be submitted to the censors before they were allowed to be released for public consumption. Of course anti-richelieu works were in circulation, but Richelieu did his best to rebut such views. In 1640 he established the 'imprimerie royale'- the royal printing press, which was based in the Louvre, hence bringing the publication of royal and ministerial materials in-house where the crown and ministers had more creative control of their work as well as benefiting economically, where costs were saved. Among the first books to be published by the new press were religious works by St Bernard, St

Louis XIV and Richelieu

Ignatius of Loyola and St Francois de Sales, all founders of the catholic orders- the Cistercians, the Jesuits, whilst the latter proved an inspiration for the Salesian order. Richelieu funded the project for the next three years by providing subsidies However, the press declined in use of the time of Richelieu and Louis xiii.

According to Sturdy, perhaps one of Richelieu's greatest legacy is the establishment of the Academie Francaise, founded in 1635- the Academie is still around today, acting as a meeting establishment for France's brights and intellectuals. The Acadamie derived its name from the Roman Academy founded by Pomponio Leto, a notable academy in renaissance Italy. As Knecht notes, the aim of the Academy was to proclaim the importance and beauty of the French language- 'a tongue as beautiful, universal and lasting as Cicero's Latin' (cf. Knecht, Richelieu). The Academy was originally a set of meetings convened by Valentin Conrart, to discuss matters of style and language (cf. Sturdy, Richelieu and Mazarin). They would discuss literature, 'read their own books to each other, exchange court gossip, go for walks, and take refreshments (cf. Knecht, Richelieu). Richelieu learnt of these group from the Abbe de Boisroberta and Jean Chapelain- two of the cardinal's friends and confidantes on literary matters. Keen to capitalise this disparate group into something more professional, Richelieu brought the institution into the arms of the state. Among its newer members were the cardinals' creatures and also two ministers of state: Abel Servien and Pierre Seguier. By 1642 the Academie was filled with a wide spectrum of talented artists- no one group monopolised the set (cf. Sturdy, Richelieu and Mazarin, Knecht, Richelieu)

According to Chapelain Richelieu required that only his servants and creatures should be members of the academy. Some of the members were used as the cardinal's speech writers, others to defend his theological treatises, whilst others were employed to write pamphlets explaining and defending the cardinal's policies (cf. Knecht, Richelieu). This has led some to criticise the Academy as little more than a political organ used by the king and his cardinal to voice out and promote their policies. One such critic Mathieu de Morgues notes:

'In truth, [he wrote] I have never seen a man more unfortunate in his eulogies than his Eminence who has never been esteemed by an upright man nor praised by an able and learned writer. He has recognised his poverty, and in order to overcome it he has established a school or rather an aviary of Psapho, the Academy…There assemble a great many poor zealots who learn to compose frauds and to disguise ugly acts and make ointments to soothe the wounds of the public and the Cardinal. He promises some advancements to and gives small favours to this

Louis XIV and Richelieu

rabble who combat truth for bread' (cf. Knecht, Richelieu, Church, Richelieu and Reason of State).

That is not strictly not true. The Academy did not only have the support of Richelieu's favourites- it contained may other authors who came from a different background and had other interests rather than just the interest of the cardinal. In that sense there were dominant parties within the Academy- all were allowed to pursue their studies in freedom, unburdened with the need to support the cardinal's professional and personal views.

Richelieu moved from a position of personal patronage of a set of powerful writers and artists to one of patronage by the state. He welcomed members of the Academie 'with so much grace, politeness, majesty and sweetness that all those present were ravished'. Such was the cardinal's reverence and support for academic freedom that he invalidated all statues requiring members of the academy to revere and praise the cardinal (cf. Knecht, Richelieu)- hence keeping their academic freedom intact. Unlike the Roman Academy, the neither the king nor the cardinal visited the Academy- that task was reserved for the Keeper of the Seals. One reason why this was so, as Knecht validly points out is that the cardinal wished to maintain the intellectual freedom that the writers had, rather than the state supporting such writers (cf. Knecht, Richelieu). Richelieu appointed Contrart as its first secretary. The

Academie patronised scholarship, painting, architecture, music and the sciences 'that was to become a distinctive feature of French cultural life' (cf. Sturdy, Richelieu and Mazarin). The Academy was to prove an important tool for many centuries to come where France used such soft power to advertise herself and promote her values on the European and world stage.

Richelieu was also interested in the aesthetic life of France. Beauty was the very incarnation of the king's 'gloire'- if you will. As Sturdy notes, Richelieu left behind an impressive architectural heritage. For Richelieu, all political figures must live in a manner befitting their importance and leave behind important buildings for posterity, The cardinal undertook three major architectural works: his residence in Paris (the 'Palais Cardinal', now occupied by the Palais Royal). The church of Sorbonne, and a new town bordering Touraine and Poitou, named after himself, Richelieu. His designer of choice for these building schemes was Jacques Lemercier, the most popular architect in the whole of France. Creatively, Lemercier combined French minimalism- 'plain exterior walls, simple windows, high-pitched roofs' combined with Roman grandeur. Richelieu's first commissioned work by Lemericier was a country house at Rueil, a stone's thruway from Saint Germain, where the king resided, but it was the Palais Cardinal, close to the Louvre, which

Louis XIV and Richelieu

presented him with a major project. In 1634, Richelieu purchased the Hotel d'Argennes, demolished said hotel and set Lemermier to begin work on its replacement. The project by 1629 had been substantially completed enough for Richelieu to take up residence, though the palace was not completed until 1639, ten years on from when Richelieu had initially moved in. When completed, it had a courtyard at the entrance whilst there was a large space at the back, where gardens, fountains and trees were located and based. The interior was filled with furniture, tapestries, paintings, statues, porcelain, silver and all other paraphanalia befitting a palatial residence. It also contained a painting gallery filled with famous men and women (the paintings were executed by Simon Vouet and Philllipe de Champaigne) and a theatre. Whilst work was still being completed on the palace, Lemercier was commissioned to design the church of the Sorbonne, funded and financed by Richelieu. Following the Greco-Roman style, the entrance had classical columns, whilst the edifice was garnished with a large dome. Richelieu also carried out improvements to his palace and cathedral based at Lucons. He was also tasked with supervising the building of the queen mother's new residence in Paris, the Luxembourg palace, hence bringing him into contact with the likes of Salomon Brosse and Charles de Ry, who were architects as well as painters and sculptors like Rubens and Berthelot (cf. Sturdy, Richelieu and Mazarin).

Richelieu was appalled at the state of his lodgings in Lucon:

'I am very poorly housed, [he wrote]...as you can see. I do not need a harsh winter; the only remedy is patience. I assure you that I have the worst bishopric in France [le plus crotte] and the most disagreeable...there is nowhere to stroll: no garden, no path, nothing, so that my house is a prison' (cf. Knecht, Richelieu).

The cathedral too was in state- it had cracked walls, its statues, paintings, tapestries and candlebra had been dispatched of- only the altars remained intact. Richelieu set out to realise improvements to his palace and contribute a third of costs to finance the improvement of the cathedral (cf. Knecht, Richelieu).

Richelieu's most ambitious project was the building of a new town based at his ancestral home. By this time he had been promoted to the post of surintendant in the household of the queen mother, Marie de Medici (cf. Bergin, Brockliss, Richelieu and his Age). Again, in 1625- he commissioned Lemercier to oversee the town to completion. The run-down chateau was transformed into an impressive, modern building. Meanwhile, Richelieu acquired more land next the chateau- his aim being to transform the familial estate of Richelieu into

Louis XIV and Richelieu

a duchy through expansion where he could received increased income and increased revenue. Richelieu was very much supported by Louis who granted him the title of 'Cardinal-duc' hence recognising and approving of Richelieu's newly formed duchy. Richelieu did not stop there- such was his ambition and desire for power- he then set out to turn the estate into a town. As well as the king, Richelieu was supported by the queen mother in his territorial ambitions. She helped him with the purchase of 'Limours ((near Fontainebleau) in 1623 and made him a gift of the Petit-Luxembourg in 1627, followed by a further gift of 180,000 livres for the purchase of Bois-le Vicomte in 1628 (cf. Bergin, Brockliss, Richelieu and his Age). According to Sturdy, Richelieu's project was not particularly successful due to its location lacking and proving to be a barrier to commercial and corporate routes (cf. Sturdy, Richelieu and Mazarin). That is not strictly true- Richelieu's territorial gains and expansion made him one of the most powerful men in France- Richelieu's territorial gains increased his presence in France and improved his economic situation, given that through his land he received a personal stream of income.

As well as attending to his own personal projects, Richelieu also assumed responsibility for works that the king wanted to see to fruition. He took charge of construction, decoration and restoration in the household of the king (cf. Bergin, Brockliss, Richelieu and his Age).

Richelieu was very much a cultured man- the most cultured man- if you will, in the whole of France. He was the creative director of the king's court and in charge if you will- of entertainment and events that occurred at the king's court. According to Margaret McGowan, from 1635, most court ballets were performed at Richelieu's charge. These included 'Le Ballet de Quatre Monarchies Chretiennes' (1635), a state of nation play- if you will; 'La Ballet de la Marine' (1635) which celebrated the birth of Louis xiv, Louis' son, the dauphin, the 'Ballet de la Prosperite des armes de la France' (1641), celebrating the union of the king's family '(through [the king's] niece Clemence de Maille-Breze) to the blood royal (through the duc d'Enghien, future Grand Conde)' 'and by no means least' according to Caldicott, 'the final superb statement of national political strategy with 'Europe (1642)' – a fin de ciecle if you will. Richelieu also sponsored the performance of ballets at the king's court (cf. Bergin, Brockliss, Richelieu and his Age).

Richelieu was also interested in sculpture. He supported two camps: French realism (for example, Thomas Boudin, Barthelemy Tremblay, Germain Gissey), as well as the more ornate Italian movement consisting of figures such as Jacques Sarrazin, Simon Guilan, Christopher Cochet and Pierre Biard. Richelieu commissioned the latter to create a bust of Louis xiii for the chateau of Limours, but soon switched to Guillaume Berthelot, who had received training in Rome before entering the service of the queen mother. The cardinal commissioned from Berthelot statues for the chateau Richelieu and for the chapel at Sorbonne.

Richelieu, according to Knecht was the first private individual to collect works of art on a large and epic scale in the whole of France. Many works survive and can be found in museums all across the world. They include Michelangelo's Slaves, paintings by Mantegna, Perugino and Lorenzo Costa that had adorned the studiolo of Isabelle d'Este. Poussin's 'Bacchanalia' and the marquetry table now in 'Galerie d'Apollon' based at the Louvre. It may have been the queen mother, Marie de Medici that sparked off his interest in art collection when she suggested to the duke of Mantua that he should send the cardinal 'some excellent pictures'. The Mantuan ambassador noted that the cardinal was 'a great collector of rare pictures'. Richelieu was gifted many times with works of art. Henri duc de Montmorency gifted him Michelangelo's 'Slaves' shortly before being dispatched of. In 1633, Alfonso Lopez, a Jewish business man asked his agent based in Provence to purchase anything 'curious and rare' so that it might be gifted to Richelieu. When

Mazarin on a trip back from Rome as nuncio in 1644 he brought items from Antonio Barberini and gifted them to the cardinal- they included four paintings by Titian, Pietro da Cortona, Guilo Romano and Antonini, respectively, a cassock, some small tables and a bureau 'full of a thousand galanteries of perfume'. Mazarin was attacked by many for using his pension to fund the cardinal's works of art who 'like a God did not want anyone to approach him empty-handed'. In terms of art collation Richelieu was in the league of the likes of the king of England, the duke of Parma and the queen mother, Marie de Medici by collating treasures form the Gonzaga collection. Richelieu was very much a renaissance man. As well as taking a personal interest and role in art collecting, he also delegated such matters to others. For example, Lord Arundel, helped him buy works of sculpture, and allowed he cardinal to acquire a collection of works from the palace in Rome and supplied the cardinal with information about eighty busts in different parts of Italy. In 1633, Cardinal Baberini, the nephew of Pope Urban viii helped Richelieu in his endeavours of purchasing works of art, often advising the cardinal as to which works to purchase. He was also assisted by his 'creatures' such as Frangipani or Mazarin. In France one of his key collaborators was the aforementioned Alfonso Lopez- another was the archbishop Sourdis who supervised works at chateau Richelieu and advised the cardinal on which works of art to pick and select. The collection of arts works at the Chateau became one of Europe's largest collection of artworks as well as hosting the largest collection of roman sculpture in France. Amongst his collection was Leonardo's 'Virgin and Child with Saint Anne', 'The Family of the Virgin' by Andrea del Sardo, the two famous 'Bacchanales' of Nicholas Poussin, as well as paintings by Veronese and Titian as well as 'Diana at the Bath' by Rubens Despite delegating, Richelieu was very much in charge of monitoring the state of his works of art- for example, in 1636 he asked for two paintings by Poussin to be brought before him at Amiens, in the midst of a military campaign, hence demonstrating his masterful command of the data of works of art (cf. Knecht, Richelieu).

Richelieu also collected valuables such as silver and jewellery often destined to be located at the Palais-Cardinal. By the end, Richelieu had 54 dozen dishes of silver or silver gilt. Within his collection there were, chandeliers, basins, salt-cellars, sweetmeat dishes, baskets, flagons, fruit bowls, ewers, nefs and buckets. The collection was valued at 237,000 livres. Ecclesiastic silver, including crosses basins, censers, aspersoria and paxes worth an additional 10,000 livres (cf. Knecht, Richelieu and Mazarin). At the chapel of the Palais-Cardinal, there were paintings which were of solid gold- crucifix, chalice, paten, ciborium, candlesticks- set and composed in 180 rubies and 9,000 diamonds (cf. Bonnaffe).

In addition to accumulating works of art, Richelieu also collected books to fill his own personal library. The manuscripts number 900, codified in red Morocco with the cardinal's arms.

Richelieu as well as collecting works of arts, opened art galleries and conducted work on the ceilings of royal palaces. This is confirmed by the work carried out on the gallery of the Palais-Cardinal by Champaigne (cf. Bergin, Brockliss, Richelieu and his Age).

According to the historian Honor Levi, 'it is in the end difficult' 'to dismiss the notion that Richelieu's collections represented so much personal aesthetic taste as a desire to publicise the external signs of the political power that nourished his soul' (cf. Knecht, Richelieu). One could note that Richelieu did his best to improve the intellectual and cultural of France which she enjoys- even to this day. France enjoys a healthy intellectual life- all of this can be attributed to the works and endeavours of du Plessis. Without du Plessis there would be no Descartes, no Diderot, no Voltaire, no Herbert Marcuse, no Deleuze, no Derrida and no Sartre for that matter (cf. Levi, Cardinal Richelieu and the Making of France)- such was du Plessis' contribution to the cultural and intellectual life of France.

CONCLUDING THOUGHTS

Towards the end of his career, relations between Richelieu and the catholic church became colder. Richelieu was angry that Pope Urban viii had refused him the role of Papal Legate of France (cf. Perkins). In turn the pope disapproved of the administration of the church in France as well as French policy against the catholic Hapsburgs. Despite these relations, Richelieu did not support the separatist Gallican movement in France and hence in that sense Richelieu was always loyal to the roman church, of which he did his best to improve.

After the Cinq-Mars affair, Louis and Richelieu became more distant from each other. A few weeks later, Richelieu was taken ill. For many years, his health had been poor and had suffered from reoccurring fevers, strangury, intestinal tuberculosis with fistula, and migraines.

Becoming nearer to death, Armand named Cardinal Mazarin as his successor to the role and post of first minister.

He passed away on 5 December 1642, aged 59. Jean Armand du Plessis was now no longer around.

In conclusion, it is fair to say that Richelieu was a transformative and important leader in the life of France.

His method of governance was to be adopted and followed by many generations of French kings and queens. Richelieu was the architect of the modern nation state where she gained a self confidence and self identity that had previously eluded her.

Richelieu was one of the first to recognise that a well organised propaganda machine was crucial to the promotion of policies within the realm, as well as a tool to generate support amongst the citizens of France by informing said citizens of governmental policies, governmental plans and the trajectory and strategy that France would take in the medium and long terms.

Through the use of his 'creatures', supporters and intendants Richelieu kept a tight leash on all within France, though he allowed said all to enjoy freedom, independence and autonomy, albeit it with respect to law and order and reverence and acknowledgement of the king's authority.

In terms of foreign policy- results are mixed. Though there were successes in the Mantuan affair and much later on after Richelieu's time where there was French success in the Thirty War, other wars such as the Swedish affair and the war against Spain were less successful. Nevertheless, Richelieu did improve the functioning and quality of the army. He also improved the navy. These military reforms were to benefit France's later international efforts of which much success was enjoyed by France as a global player and global power.

Richelieu was intensely loyal to Louis, his king and above all to France. What France gave him, he too gave them back more, such was his love for and loyalty to king and country.

Du Plessis turned France into a global power and a key player and country in the European and western world which was to last for generations to come, which has lasted France even to the present day.

In a sense Richelieu set the pattern and style for other European countries to follow. His style and model of governance was set to influence other European countries and other western countries. For that we must be grateful to Armand Jean du Plessis Cardinal Richelieu.

BIBLIOGRAPHY

Primary sources
Andre, Testament Politique

Secondary sources
Knecht, Richelieu
Sturdy, Richelieu and Mazarin
Bergin and Brockliss, Richelieu and his Age
Bergin, The Rise of Richelieu
Bergin, Cardinal Richelieu, power and pursuit of wealth
Levi, Cardinal Richelieu and the Making of France
Treasure, Cardinal Richelieu and the Development of Absolutism
Wedgwood, Richelieu and the French Monarchy

Lightning Source UK Ltd.
Milton Keynes UK
UKHW010641250722
406332UK00002B/282